THE
EDUCATION PROBLEM
IN
INDIA

THE EDUCATION PROBLEM IN INDIA

GOOROODAS BANERJEE

GYAN

Published by

GYAN

Gyan Publishing House
5, Ansari Road
Daryaganj, New Delhi-110002
Phone: 011-47034999, 9811692060
E-mail: books@gyanbooks.com

Distribution Network
gyanbooks.com
India, USA, Canada, UK, Australia

ISBN: 978-93-7133-658-1 (HB)
First Published, 1914

2nd Impression 2025

Printed at: Gyan Press, Delhi.

THE EDUCATION PROBLEM IN INDIA
Author Gooroodas Banerjee

THE EDUCATION PROBLEM IN INDIA

BY

SIR GOOROO DASS BANERJEE KT., M.A., D.L., PH.D.,
SOMETIME VICE-CHANCELLOR OF THE CALCUTTA UNIVERSITY,
FORMERLY ASSISTANT LECTURER ON MATHEMATICS IN THE
PRESIDENCY COLLEGE, CALCUTTA, AND AFTERWARDS,
LECTURER ON MATHEMATICS AND LAW IN
THE BERHAMPUR COLLEGE

S. K. LAHIRI AND CO.
56, COLLEGE STREET, CALCUTTA.
1914

PREFACE.

Many questions relating to educational reform are now engaging the attention of the Government and the public. It may not therefore be deemed inopportune to offer for consideration the few suggestions contained in the following pages, bearing on the Education Problem in India.

NARIKELDANGA, GOOROODASS BANERJEE.

the 15th November, 1914

TABLE OF CONTENTS.

CHAPTER V.

CHAPTER VI.

The Education Problem in India

INTRODUCTORY REMARKS.

Object aimed at—to offer suggestions for improvement.—The object of the following pages is to offer a few practical suggestions for the improvement of the system of Education in this country in its different branches, and not to present any theoretical disquisition on educational topics.

As my suggestions relate to matters, many, if not most, of which are of a controversial character, theoretical discussion will often be unavoidable, for the purpose of shewing that the suggestions are sound. But such discussion will be only subsidiary to the main object stated above, and no part of the object itself.

Method of treatment.—That being the object aimed at, the method of treatment should be such as would help its attainment. A speculative treatise on Education may expand into refined and lengthy disquisition which leisured men of thought may have time to read; but a paper of practical suggestions intended for busy men of action, should be as concise as possible, consistently with clearness, as otherwise they may not find time to read it even if they feel any inclination to do so.

Moreover, as many of my suggestions will not fall in with generally accepted views, and as some initial repugnance towards them on the part of my readers will be inevitable, I must not add to my difficulty by making my remarks unpleasant. I have no quarrel with men. I shall only oppose their measures, and even in doing so, I shall avoid criticizing with undue severity any cherished though unsound views of esteemed but erring friends, and respected but misguided administrators. My tone will be considerate, but not compromising; for to be compromising in such cases would be to trifle with truth.

There are two difficulties which I must anticipate and be prepared for, one arising from the attitude of experts, and the other from that of officials, towards suggestions proceeding from non-experts and non-officials.

Those who are, or consider themselves to be, experts, show, as a rule, very little consideration to the opinions of those who are not; and this is true in a marked degree of educational experts. I do not wonder at this. I think it is but natural that they who have devoted special attention to a subject should regard others who have not done so, incompetent to give them advice, and should consider themselves quite competent to act without advice; and educational experts, that is professors and teachers who have chiefly to work with their inferiors in learning, have this feeling of self-sufficiency developed to an inordinate extent. There are exceptions and sometimes noble exceptions to this, and scholars whose culture and experience would fully justify their self-sufficiency, are found to be most considerate towards the views of others. To them I have nothing to say here. But to the more exclusive and less tolerant among their colleagues I would make an earnest appeal asking them to remember that outsiders may sometimes find out real flaws and suggest useful improvements, as "standers-by discover blots, which are apt to escape those who are in the game".

And if experts from a sense of conscious superiority are disinclined to listen to non-experts, officials are not less so, to receive suggestions from non-officials, for the same reason, and, as is sometimes supposed, also for another reason, namely, an apprehension lest official prestige should suffer by yielding to public demand. But there is no reason for any such apprehension. The doctor does not suffer in public estimation if he asks his patient for information as to the nature of the ailment, and if he changes his prescription to suit any altered circumstances. No more will an official suffer in prestige if he alters his measures on finding, upon information from those for whom the measures were intended, that they have not worked well. When advice is given with ostentatious obtrusiveness, it may merit unceremonious rejection. But when suggestions are submitted respectfully and earnestly with all becoming diffidence, they deserve better treatment than what they often receive. And I may here state for the information of our administrators, that considering the temperament of the Indian people, who have greater respect for reason than for power, official prestige will be enhanced and not diminished in this country, if people find that those in authority are ready to modify their measures if only they are satisfied that reason requires such modification.

I have laboured a little over these preliminary points on account of their vital importance. It rests mainly with educational experts and officials to give effect to my suggestions; and unless they are received, I do not say with favour, for that will depend upon their intrinsic merit, but without repugnance, which is the outcome of extrinsic circumstances, they will be practically useless.

I am not sure whether the course I have adopted in seeking to remove that repugnance by pointing out its causes, is a prudent one. But I am sure of this, that in commenting upon the sources of prejudice I have not been actuated by any fault-finding spirit. I have referred to the sources of prejudice only to account for its existence, which I have freely admitted to be but natural. And I am sure also of this, that one of the best modes of preventing a well-regulated mind from yielding to prejudice is to point out its possible existence and the causes from which it arises, so that it may be guarded against. If I may not hope to have removed prejudice by referring to its sources, I do hope to have avoided offending any susceptibilities by doing so.

If the truth of the propositions I intend to propound admitted of mathematical demonstration, I would not have paused to combat prejudice at the out-set, but would have proceeded to state my views at once, leaving them to find such reception as the reasons in their favour entitled them to deserve. But that is not the nature of my subject. Mathematical certainty here is unattainable, and it is possible for two disputants both earnestly seeking after truth, to maintain opposite views upon one and the same question. This is due to two causes. In the first place, though the main reasons for and against any view may be enumerated with accuracy, it is not easy to make the enumeration exhaustive, and some weighty reasons on one side or the other may escape attention. And in the second place, even if the enumeration of conflicting considerations be fairly complete, it is by no means easy to make a correct estimate of the weight to be attached to each. To one mind a certain consideration will appeal with great force, while to another its weight may be insignificant. So that a qualitative statement of the reasons for and against a view may or may not be exhaustively complete, and a quantitative statement of the weight to be attached to each reason cannot be exactly correct. It is thus that prejudice or antecedent predilection of the mind becomes a potent factor in determining its decision, each mind attaching to conflicting considerations such weight as its previous training and habits of thought may incline it to do. Hence the combating of prejudice becomes as necessary as it is difficult.

Different heads of the subject. Before proceeding to offer my suggestions, I shall mention the different heads under which I intend to treat this discourse. It will be a mere enumeration of the heads for practical convenience, and not a classification of them on any logical principle.

I. Statement of the Education Problem and of a few Fundamental Principles.

I shall begin with a statement of the Education Problem for the solution of which I am submitting my suggestions. I shall state also concisely and categorically a few Fundamental Principles the truth of which will be assumed throughout this discussion.

II. Different Kinds of Education.

I shall next deal with the different Kinds of Education that ought to be imparted, with a few general remarks appropriate to each.

III. Control of Education.

My next point for discussion will be the Control of Education.

IV. Organization of a System of Education.

I shall then deal with the Organization of a System of Education.

V. Methods of Imparting Education.

That will be followed by a consideration of the Methods of Imparting Education.

VI. Modes of Testing Education.

And lastly, I shall deal with the Methods of Testing Education.

CHAPTER I.

Statement of the Education Problem and of a few Fundamental Principles.

Statement of the Education Problem.

The Education Problem may be shortly stated thus :—

To determine how to impart Education in its different branches so as to secure the greatest attainable benefit at the least cost of time, energy, and money.

This statement requires some explanation.

In the first place the meaning of the expression 'different branches' of education should be definitely explained. In the second place, the mode of estimating the greatest attainable benefit of education should be clearly explained. And lastly, the principle on which the cost of education in time, energy and money ought to be assessed and apportioned should also be explained. With proper explanation of these points, the statement set out above may be taken to be a fair statement of the Education Problem.

The first point may be left to be dealt with in detail under the second head of my discourse, and it will be sufficient for purposes of explanation to say that the different branches of Education, contemplated in the problem are,—

I. Physical Education.

II. Intellectual Education including—

(1) General Education in its three different stages,—Primary, Secondary, and Collegeate.

(2) Professional Education, including Education in Law, Medicine, and Engineering.

(3) Technical Education, including Education in Agriculture, Manufacture and Commerce.

III. Moral Education.

IV. Religious Education.

On the second point, it should be noted that, much as we may wish to secure the benefits of Education to an unlimited extent, the circumstances of each community impose limits beyond which it is not possible to go immediately, though we should arrange matters so as to make gradual advance easy in the near future. My saying this must not be taken to imply any assent to the erroneous and mischievous doctrine that as the Indians do not belong to the White Races their progress in Education must be slower than its progress among those races. The doctrine is erroneous, because the fact it assumes, namely, that the Hindus do not belong to the Aryan race, has not been proved, and the inference it draws that the brain and intellect of the Indian are inferior to those of the European is not supported by evidence and is disproved to some extent by experience. And I consider the doctrine mischievous, because it has done much harm to the cause of Education by furnishing indolent teachers with an easy explanation of their ill success, and thereby proving an indirect deterrent to earnest exertion in teaching.

The real reason why education has made such slow progress in modern India is because, the country is so large, the population is so sparse, and the people are so poor. We cannot therefore expect to expand the area or raise the level of Primary Education at once, though we must do something to take the work in hand and lay the foundation for its gradual progress in the near future. The level of Technical Education also must be left to rise slowly, as there is so small investment of Indian capital for manufacture, and as foreign capitalists naturally disfavour Indian skilled labour except of the lowest sort.

In Secondary Education, in Collegiate or Higher Education, and in Professional Education, we may raise the level sufficiently high. But we should proceed gradually, because, if we raise the height suddenly, we shall reduce the base very much, so that though we may benefit the few, it will be at the expense of the many; and in the result the greatest attainable benefit will not be secured. While everything should be done to help the more gifted intellects to carry on research in order to add to the stock of human knowledge, nothing should be left undone to enable the less gifted to take their share in the already acquired stock of that knowledge. If it is the highest object of Education to train men who can add to the stock of our knowledge, it is no unworthy object of it to raise the average level of knowledge in the community, especially in a country like India where that level still stands so low. The temple of learning should be like a pyramid rising majestic on its ample base, and not like an obelisk standing high but on a narrow basis.

The third point, namely, how to adjust the cost of Education most economically, becomes a most important part of the Education Problem, owing to our resources in time, energy and money being so limited.

Neither the Vedic 'hundred autumns' nor even the Biblical 'three score years and ten' is vouchsafed unto many; and though we always live to learn, the time which one can devote exclusively to receiving Education must, remembering how many other things man has to do, be a very limited portion of his short and uncertain life. The State imposes an arbitrary age limit for admission to its service, and Nature herself imposes an age limit, less arbitrary, but no less effective, after which our power of adapting ourselves physically and mentally to the different branches of her service, no longer exists. The period of study should not therefore be protracted unreasonably.

If the time available for exclusive devotion to study is limited, the energy physical and mental, that is available for the same purpose, is not less so. I do not mean to say that the Indian student is inferior to the student in any other country, but I think the average student in any country can put forth only a limited amount of energy for acquiring knowledge or skill. The average level of Education must be raised, but the rise should be gradual, and proceed along with the gradual progress of society, so that a good portion of our common knowledge and skill may be acquired without conscious effort. We must not, therefore, seek suddenly to raise the average standard of Education unduly high.

But if the time and energy to be spent in receiving Education are so limited, still more limited are the pecuniary resources of the student in this country. In other countries where students are less poor than in India, deficiency in time and energy is sought to be compensated by sufficiency of funds wherewith to obtain all necessary help from competent teachers. In this country, the poverty of the student and the poverty of educational institutions generally, make such help unattainable. And this increases the difficulty of the Education Problem in India very considerably.

Statement of a few Fundamental Principles.—I have given above a fair statement of the problem to be solved, with some indication of the difficulties attending its solution. Before proceeding to state the suggestions that occur to me for dealing with the problem successfully, I shall try to formulate a few fundamental propositions the truth of which will be assumed in the following discussion. In thus formulating what may be regarded as the axioms on which my arguments will be based, I must not be supposed to be pedantically imitating the method followed in Spinoza's Geometrical Ethics or in Whewell's Mechanical Euclid. My object in laying down the following propositions at the outset is, simply to state once for all with necessary explanation certain principles the truth of which will be assumed in different places, with a view to avoid repetition, and to enable my reader to have a better opportunity of discovering any weak points in the basis of my suggestions.

(i) **Principle of Simplicity.**—The principle which I would state first of all is, what I may call the Principle of Simplicity. It may be shortly stated thus:

In framing any scheme or formulating any rules, simplicity in point of both matter and form should be observed as far as the subject dealt with, and our power of expression, will allow.

This principle seems to be so simple, and its propriety is so self-evident, that it is readily admitted in theory; and yet, paradoxical as it may seem, that is the very reason why it is so easily disregarded in practice, and schemes are often framed and rules made, by unquestionably able men, which are found a little later to involve difficulty in their working by reason of their complexity.

One reason why this principle, so readily admitted in theory, is so easily disregarded in practice, is, that it is liable to be lost sight of owing to other and more obtrusive principles engaging attention more forcibly. In the conflict of demands on our attention, the regard shown to principles like regard shown to persons, often depends upon their more or less exacting natures, and we show more regard to the more obtrusive though less important, than to the more important but less obtrusive, in the one case as in the other.

But apart from the above reason which may seem somewhat subtle, there are other and more tangible reasons why this should be so. Though we all want simplicity, the affairs of the world are so complex and are so rapidly advancing in complexity, that the subject matter to be treated in any case does not easily admit of being dealt with in a simple manner.

The very definition of progress, according to one eminent philosopher, is change from the homogeneous to the heterogeneous. To make any scheme or rule meet all the diverse cases that varying conditions may give rise to, its framers have to introduce qualifications and exceptions, provisos and paranthetical clauses, which must complicate its statement and clog its operation. And the limitations on our power of expression, the imperfections of language, add not a little to our difficulty. Then again, this characteristic of progress, this change from the homogeneous to the heterogeneous, has a powerful indirect effect on the mind, which catches the contagion and considers nothing in keeping with progress, unless it is cumbrous and complex and involves a dignified difficulty of being understood at once. There are some minds and able minds too, that actually revel in complications.

But if this change from the homogeneous to the heterogeneous, from the one to the many, be the sign of progress in the external world of matter, a change in the reverse order from the heterogeneous back again to the homogeneous, from the many back again to the one, has no less been the sign of progress in the internal world of mind. The highest aim of science has been to classify diverse units into connected groups and to discover comprehensive general laws governing multifarious particular phenomena.

Nor should we forget that complicated machinery, however admirable to look at when working well, is often liable to get out of gear and does not wear well in the long run.

To shew that in thus combating complexity I am not fighting with a shadow, I may refer to an instance which is only one out of many. The Calcutta University Regulations for the Matriculation Examination require (see Chapter XXX, Calender for 1911 Part I. page 140) that in order to pass the Examination, a candidate must obtain

"In English either:—

In the first paper 40 marks and in the aggregate of the two papers 72 marks; or in the aggregate of the two papers 80 marks."

The first paper is in English Translation from a vernacular and in English Essay writing, and the second is in Explanation of passages in English and in English Grammar, each paper carrying 100 marks. It is certainly desirable that a student should acquire greater proficiency in writing English than in explaining passages and understanding grammatical niceties; and so the rule fixes the minimum pass marks in the first paper at 4 per cent higher than the average that is 36 per cent in each or 72 out of 200 in the aggregate, and allows a lower minimum in the first paper to be compensated only by a still higher average minimum than 36, that is, by an average minimum of 40 per cent. Tne rule is sound in theory, but it is very cumbrous in practice, and involves great difficulty in the tabulation of results, the publication of which is delayed in consequence, when several thousand candidates have to be examined. And after all, the question remains whether the additional 4 per cent of the marks practically secures the proficiency which we want, and is worth the additional trouble which it costs.

But I fear in advocating simplicity I am plunging into prolixity, and I must here stop.

(ii) **Principle of Parsimony**—My second principle which I may call the Principle of Parsimony, may be stated thus:—

The rules to be laid down on any subject should be as small in number as possible, and no rule should be laid down unless it is required for securing some substantial good which cannot be otherwise attained, or for preventing some real evil which cannot be otherwise avoided.

Rules on any subject should be simple not only when taken singly, but also when taken collectively; that is, there should be no needless multiplication of rules.

Rules are framed no doubt for the salutary purpose of defining, and securing observance of, some desirable line of conduct; but their operation is liable to lead to certain evils. In the first place, every rule interferes with freedom of action which should be encouraged as far as possible. And in the second place, every rule is liable to be evaded, and attempts at evasion are not only bad in themselves but lead to worse results in the shape of manufacture of devices to help evasion and prevent detection.

When things left to themselves are, by the operation of natural causes, likely to work well, or even fairly well, it is doubtful policy to try to help Nature by artificial rules. Then again, where the reason of a rule is not easily discoverable, it fails to secure willing obedience and runs the risk of evasion in a more than ordinary degree. The framer of every rule should see how far the good to be secured by its operation would outweigh the attendant evils, and compensate the cost in time, energy and money to ensure its observance.

I may here give an instance of a rule, apparently harmless, but really attended with much evil in its operation. I mean the rule which requires that a candidate for the Matriculation Examination of the Calcutta University must be above the age of 16 years.

It is good to discourage enforced precocity; it is good also to have an early age record of every one receiving Education. But it is an evil to prevent a boy who is able and willing to do so, from proceeding with his educational career because he has not satisfied an arbitrary hard and fast rule requiring him to complete to the exactness of a day a certain age on a certain date. And the extent of the evil will be realized when we bear in mind the circumstances of our students. There is no regular practice of registering birth in the case of Hindus, and the age of a Hindu boy when first admitted to school is often given by guess. When the importance of the pcint is perceived and the exact age is found on enquiry to satisfy the requirement of the University Regulation, the candidate is met by the difficulty arising from disagreement between his correct age and the age recorded in the school admission register. This is sought to be explained by affidavits, but the University authorities, naturally enough, generally prefer accepting the age recorded in the school admission register as correct. Thus the operation of the rule may often possibly involve injustice to the student, and it does always certainly entail the trouble of a quasi-judicial inquiry on the authorities of the school and the University. All this might be avoided by abolishing the rule fixing the age limit, which is not really needed. There is a natural guarantee against boys who are too young being as a rule prepared to appear at the Matriculation Examination. In the exceptional cases in which such boys are prepared to appear at that examination, there is no harm done to any one if they are allowed to appear. Parental care may be safely trusted to prevent any enforcement of precocity. And as for having an age record, such record may be kept without fixing any age limit for appearing at any examination.

(iii) Principle of Justice.

If it is desirable that any body of rules to be laid down on any subject should be simple and short so that they may be understood and worked out with ease,

It is necessary that all rules should in themselves be, and should be perceived by those whom they concern to be, perfectly just, so that they may be accepted and submitted to with alacrity.

That is how I would enunciate my third general principle, that is, the Principle of Justice. No one will deny the truth of this principle, but almost every one will, I fear, deny the necessity of its formal enunciation, and many may consider it impertinence on my part to give it a prominent insertion in this place. I have done this with much diffidence, and not without some reason.

I need hardly say that my doing this does not carry with it the slightest implication that the framers of our educational schemes and rules will knowingly and deliberately do any thing that is unjust. They are all enlightened and intelligent gentlemen who earnestly seek to do what is good for the great Empire of which India is a part, and I can not believe, and I think it would be un-reasonable to believe, that they would consciously do what is wrong. And yet it may happen, as it does happen, that they may be mistaken in their views as to what is right and just, and so they may be led to do what is not just, under an erroneous belief that it is. The abstract principles of justice are simple, but in their application to concrete cases great differences of opinion may arise.

Slavery was considered justifiable in cultured Greece and Christian Europe, and the cruel code of punishments in English law had its advocates in quite recent times among some of the greatest sages of that law. And it is no wonder, differences of opinion regarding justice in its concrete application should exist in a heterogeneous community like that of India, with its differences of thought, sentiment, habits and traditions.

To show that I am not drawing upon imagination, I may refer to one notable instance, namely, the scheme that

that divides Educational Service into the two sections, Indian and Provincial, the former carrying higher emoluments and privileges than the latter, and being reserved as a rule for Englishmen, Indians being admitted to it only by way of exception. And it often happens that though an Indian is in point of ability and attainments quite equal to his European colleague in the service, and does quite as important and as difficult work, yet he is placed in the lower grade and is treated as an inferior man. This is hardly just, and yet it is allowed to remain as the rule. And why? Not because Englishmen are so selfish that they want all good things of the service for themselves. No, that is not so, and in seeking justice for my countrymen I must not do injustice to Englishmen. The reason why the unjust rule stands is because it is not considered unjust. It is said that the object of our system of Education should be to train the Indian in the Western method, and that it is necessary for the attainment of that object that the work of training should be entrusted chiefly to those who have been nursed in that method from birth. Then it is said that Englishmen by their active and energetic habits are better able to maintain order and discipline than Indian teachers. And lastly it is urged that Englishmen serving in India have to work in an uncongenial climate and under many disadvantages, for which they are justly entitled to higher remuneration and greater privileges than an Indian. But it will be found on examination that the first two reasons are unsound, and the last only partially sound.

The true aim of a system of Education for Indians with their inherited and cherished habits, sentiments and traditions (many of which are good and deserve preservation) should be, not to convert them completely into Europeans (even if the habits, sentiments and traditions of the latter were all good without exception), but to make them possess all that is good in European character, and at the same time retain all that is good in their own. For such a purpose, an Indian well trained in Western method will, as a rule, be a better teacher than a European ignorant of Indian modes of thought.

In matters of experimental research and technological training, and in many other matters, the help of competent European teachers will no doubt be of the highest value. But they do not exhaust the whole subject of Education.

On the question of the supposed superiority of he Englishman over the Indian in maintaining order and discipline, conceding for the moment that the former is more active and energetic than the latter, it does not follow that that makes him more competent to maintain order and discipline in the quiet le cture room with mild Indian students. Indeed the very excess of activity and energy that is sometimes called into play, produces the reverse of the desired effect with the Indian student, whose reverence for his teacher makes him readily submit to his authority when exercised with love, but whose sensitive nature resents any unfeeling severity of treatment.

The third reason given to justify the unequal treatment of Europeans and Indians in the Education service, is sound, but is only partially so; for it will not jusfify inequality to the extent it now exists. Englishmen serving in India far away from their home, and living amidst surroundings not congenial to them, may justly claim as compensation better terms regarding pay, pension, and furlough, than those accorded to Indians, but that does not justify their being treated as superior to those Indians who are equal to them in ability and attainments. And the excess of pay that may be allowed, should be given not as part of substantive pay but as compensation for service in a distant country.

But the difficulty lies deeper, and though apparent equality may be sought to be obtained by rules, real equality of treatment cannot be secured so long as there is in the mind of the European a feeling that he is superior to the Indian as a man. I do not say that all men are equal. That is not true. But it is certainly true that no man, however high he may be intellectually or morally, should despise any other man however low. Individual superiority or inferiority is the product of heredity and a variety of other factors over which the individual has very little control; and so, for such superiority or inferiority very little personal credit or discredit can be attached to him. The superior man, or strictly speaking the man more favoured by Nature, should receive respect from the less favoured man by reason of his greater power of doing good; and if that respect is to continue, he should exercise that power not with compassionate contempt but with considerate care; while on the other hand, the inferior man, if he is to deserve the considerate care of his more favoured fellow man, should show him respect and not bear spite towards him. All that lies in our power should be done to favour the growth and interchange of salutary feelings, and to discourage the growth of their reverse, in order to enable us to do effective justice to a heterogeneous community like that in India.

Then again, not only should our rules be just, but care should be taken to make people perceive that they are just, so that they may receive willing obedience. If it is desirable that in every department of human affairs rules made should be willingly obeyed, it is more than desirable,—it is absolutely necessary,—in the field of Education, that that should be so. The administrator's work may be said to be done, though not fully done, if he can secure outward obedience to his rules, whatever the inward feelings of those obeying them may be; but the educator's work cannot be said to be half-done or even commenced, until he is able, not only to obtain outward obedience to his rules, but also to influence the inward springs of action in favour of such obedience. And for that purpose, he must take pains to convince those with whom he has to deal that his rules are just and should be obeyed.

(IV). Principle of Moderation :—

The fourth and last preliminary principle I would formulate, may be called the Principle of Moderation, and may be stated thus :—

While the ideals we set before us should be as lofty as possible, the steps designed towards attaining those ideals should be gradual and planned with moderation so as to avoid making them ambitiously high; or embarrassingly low, and with a view to obtain a maximum of result and not merely the maximum of any one factor of it.

It should be borne in mind that rules are made not for the exceptionally intelligent or the exceptionally stupid, The former will always get on, and the latter never will, whatever our rules may be. These extreme cases require exceptional treatment. It is for the large average mean of intelligence that rules are made. It is students of fair ordinary intelligence whose progress may be helped or hindered by rules, according as the rules are good or bad. The real progress of such students will be helped, not by proceeding too fast and imposing work that is too hard or too heavy, but by advancing gradually and setting task moderate in quantity and not very stiff in quality. And yet we find experienced teachers of important schools which ought to serve as models to other institutions, acting in utter disregard of this principle, and setting for boys home task which they cannot possibly get through unaided, and which is really done, not by them, but for them by their private tutors. This can do no good to students, and it does them positive harm by gradually deadening their desire and capacity to work for themselves and making them wholly dependent on their private tutors for help.

If going to one extreme is injurious to progress, going to the other extreme is not less so. For proceeding too slow and setting too iight and too easy work for students has the ssme effect of deadening their desire and capacity for work through want of proper exercise.

There is another form in which disregard of moderation manifests itself, and produces its evil effects. That is where enthusiasm for improvement in one direction makes us overlook improvement in other directions, and so we obtain the maximum of only one factor in the result and not the maximum result itself. This antagonism of different factors which go to make up the result is not an uncommon thing in life, and the problem which is somewhat similar to maxima minima problems in mathematics, is to determine the values of the different factors which will give the maximum result.

To take a familiar example by way of illustration, suppose we wish to inscribe the triangle of maximum area within a given circle. If we confine our attention to the altitude, one of the two factors on which the area depends, and take the longest line in the circle that is a diameter for the altitude, the base and with it the triangle will vanish. If we take a diameter for the base, the other factor on which the area depends, we shall have a triangle, but not the greatest. It is the triangle with equal sides that has, as we know, the greatest area. So in the affairs of life, where we have to work within a limited circle, ambition to attain the greatest altitude often altogether defeats itself. A less ambitious attempt to secure the greatest base, though not so fruitless, does not give us the greatest result either. It is only when we proceed looking equally on all sides, that we may hope to obtain the maximum result. In the field of Education, working within the limitations imposed by human imperfections in the pupil and the preceptor, our system will fail, as did that of the Middle Ages in most cases, if we unduly increase the strictness of discipliue, which is a necessary element in all training; and it will equally fail, as does that of the Froebelians in many cases, if we unduly increase the latitude of action which also is an important element in training. The object of all training being to make the capricious and unregulated will of the learner to control and regulate itself in the end, by accustoming it to be controlled and regulated by the steady and trained will of the preceptor. in the beginning some strictness of control is necessary and cannot be dispensed with because it causes pain; and on the other hand, if the pupil is to be trained to become a self-reliant man and not a machine to be worked by the preceptor, some latitude of action must be given to him, but should not be unduly increased even though it gives pleasure. How to fix the limits of these conflicting but necessary elements of strictness and latitude, is the problem for the solution of which each case has to be separately considered, and the only general rule that can be laid down is that we should avoid extremes and proceed with moderation.

CHAPTER II.

Different Kinds of Education.

I now come to the second head of my discourse, namely, the Different Kinds of Education which our system should include. These will be considered here only in a preliminary way, with a few general remarks on each, giving a comprehensive view of the system as a whole, which should be kept before the eye in dealing with the other heads; and particular suggestions relating to each kind of Education will be made later in their proper places.

The different kinds of Education which our system should include, may be arranged, with a view to convenience of treatment and not to strictness of logical classification, under the following heads:

I. Physical Education

II. Intellectual Education, comprising

- (1) General Education in its different stages of
  - (*a*) Primary,
  - (*b*) Secondary,
  - (*c*) Collegiate or Higher.
- (2) Professional Education in
  - (*a*) Law,
  - (*b*) Medicine,
  - (*c*) Engineering.
- (3) Technical Education in
  - (*a*) (*i*) Agriculture and
    - (*ii*) Mining,
  - (*b*) Manufacture,
  - (*c*) Commerce.

III. Moral Education.

IV. Religious Education.

Under head II, the distinction between (1) and (2) is well marked and well recognized. That between (2) and (3) is perhaps not so well marked nor so well recognized, and it may be said that Education in Agriculture and Commerce should rank as Professional Education. But nevertheless (3) is a distinct group by itself, its sub-heads (a) and (b) relating to the production of wealth in the shapes of raw materials and finished articles respectively, and its head (c) relating to the distribution and exchange of wealth.

I shall now make a few general remarks on each of the different heads mentioned above.

I. Physical Education.

With regard to Physical Education, I shall make only two suggestions.

In the first place, Physical Education should include only such education and training as may be calculated to make our students healthy human beings, and not athletes or acrobats.

In the second place, Physical training should not be made compulsory. The element of compulsion will deprive it of the attendant feeling of pleasure without which it will fail to be conducive to health.

II. Intellectual Education.

I come next to the consideration of Intellectual Education.

The sub heads of (1) are well recognized, though it is not easy to draw the exact dividing lines between (a) and (b) and between (b) and (c).

(1) *General Education.* (*a*) *Primary.*—Beginning with General Education, and the first stage of it, namely, the Primary, it is clear that here as in most other cases, extension and comprehension must vary in inverse proportion. If we

wish Primary Education to reach any very large extent of the population, its curriculum cannot be made very comprehensive, for there are not many who can give their children education that would cost much in time, energy, and money. As it is certainly desirable that absolute illiteracy should not exist in any part of the population, and every one should be able to read, write, and make easy calculations, my first suggestion with regard to Primary Education is that its curriculum should be of a very limited character in order that it may extend as nearly as possible over the entire population.

My suggestions in detail as to the curriculum of studies for Primary, Secondary, and Higher Education, will be given in their proper place under the head of Organization of a System of Education.

There is one question of principle (and not of detail) in connection with Primary Education. regarding which a few remarks may be made in this place, namely, the question whether Primary Education should be made compulsory. Considering the very great desirability of making every one learn to read and write, and the equally great improbability of poor parents, who form the majority of the population in this country, giving their children even that modicum of general Education unless they are compelled to do so, enthusiastic social and educational reformers are for making Primary Education compulsory, and for having a law which should punish, though lightly, every father who without allowable excuse (to be defined by law) neglects to send his children to school, when there is a school within a certain distance. At one time I shared the same view. But further consideration has convinced me that, strong as are the reasons urged by these enthusiastic reformers, there are equally strong reasons the other way. The power of punishing people for not sending their children to school will be abused in many cases; poor parents will be sorely tempted to fabricate false excuses in many others; and a system of compulsory Primary Education will often add more to the miseries of the poor than the blessings of such Education can add to their happiness. I would therefore hesitate to advocate compulsory Primary Education. But at the same time, I am not in favour of absolute inaction in the matter. I would suggest, that a legislative enactment or a Government resolution may be passed, requiring the appropriation of a portion of the revenue of each Province to Primary Education, for establishing free primary schools, and that people may be encouraged to send their children to school by the offer of reward in the shape of privilege to vote at municipal elections even when not possessing the necessary property qualification, if they have children attending school or children who have finished their Primary Education. The grant of such privilege within proper limits is not likely to lead to any harm, and may be expected to work well.

In regard to (*b*) *Secondary Education* the standard should be high, but moderately high, as otherwise the extent it will reach will be proportionately narrow. The question how far the height can be raised without materially reducing the base, and thereby materially affecting the extent of Education in a community, is in the nature of a maxima minima problem the solution of which is by no means easy. Nor must we, in considering the question, forget that human society is progressive, and that the standard of Education should always go on advancing in order to help social progress. But at the same time it should be borne in mind that the progress of society is indicated, not by any nominally great raising of the standard of Education which can be availed of only by a few, but by the real rise of the general level of knowledge in the community; and such rise must be gradual, the advance at each step being moderate, and resting upon the safe and settled basis of previous advance already well made.

(*c*) *Higher Education* should have two limits, one moderately high, and marking the standard for an ordinary or a Pass Degree, the other rising much higher and marking successively the standard's for Honours and the Master's and Doctor's Degrees. To satisfy the honest ambition of a moderately gifted member of the community to attain the rank of an ordinary University Graduate, it is desirable that the standard for a Pass Degree should be only moderately high. That will not lower the standard of Education or prove injurious to the interests of Educatoin in any way, if the standards for Honours and for higher Degrees are maintained sufficiently high. On the contrary it will help the spread of Educatoin and dissemination of knowledge, by offering inducement for study to the moderately gitted who form the majority in every commnoity.

The standards of (2) *Professioual Education* should be fixed sufficiently high, commensurate with the responsibilities which those declared qualified will have to discharge. And the standard of Technical Education in its different brancbes should be determined in view of the work which those receiving such Education wtll have practially to undertake. A modicum of general knowledge is useful and necessary in every branch of Technical Education, and the standard of Agricultural Education in India should be fixed with special reference to Indian soil and Indian surroundings, and not with reference to agriculture in cold climates.

III. Moral Education.

While Intellectual Education aims at qualifying men to do well their parts in their respective spheres of life, Moral Educaiion is iutended to qualiify men to live as human beings should live, whatever their vocation in life may be. Moral Education is therefore necessary for all men in ail spheres of life. Then again Moral Education consists not in the teaching of moral truths alone, but also in training the learner to live according to those truths. Happily for man, the elementery truths of morality are simpie and can be easily known ; but unhappily for man, it is most difficult to live according to those truths. Hence arises the necessity of Moral Education.

IV. Religious Education.

Religious Education is a very difficult and delicate snbject, especialy in India with its diversity of sects and races. But amidst all this diversity of creeds, there is unity in almost all of them upon two important points. They all or almost all admit the existence of God, and and the existence of a future state. And it is this unity of all religions that makes Religious Education practicable.

Female Education and National Education are two other Heads and not *Kinds* of Education.

Female Education includes Education of every sort through all its stages adapted to the requirements of females, assuming their requirements to be different in some respects from those of males.

National Education includes Education of evry sort through all its stages, adapted to the requirements of a nation.

CHAPTER III

Control of Education.

The questions that arise for considaration under the third Head of my discourse, namely, the Control of Education, are,

(1) What are the different kinds of control that may be exercised?

(2) Where should such control rest? And how should it be exercised?

(1) As to different kinds of control.

In any complicated system like that of Education with its divers logical and local divisions, it cannot be expected that one general control will be sufficient to regulate the whole. Each ultimate part will require separate control: these separate controlling agencies in groups again will have to be controlled by some higher agency for each group; and so on, until we come to the final and highest control of the supreme power. Thus, taking as an example, the case of Higher General Education, the College which is the ultimate unit, will have to be controlled by its Principal or its governing body; Colleges affiliated to a University will be controlled by that University; Universities again under the same Local Government will be controlled by the Local Government; and finally Local Governments in their educational work will be controlled by the Supreme Government.

Thus the different kinds of control are, *first*, the *immediate* and direct control over the ultimate working unit, namely. the School or College, *second*, certain intermediate grades of *mediate* and indirect control; *third*, the final control of the State.

There are certain educational agencies, such as Medical Schools, Allopathic and Homœopathic, and the National

Council of Education, which are unconnected with Government and the Universities; and the question may arise, how far they are rightly subject to Government control.

In an educational system of the most primitive type, which can hardly be called a system, in which each ultimate working unit or school consists of a single teacher and his pupils, and where each school works separately and independently, no control immediate or mediate is necessary. But in an educational system under modern conditions, where the ultimate units, whether schools or colleges, are composed of teachers of different subjects, and where those units form organized groups working in concert, control both immediate and mediate is necessary to regulate their work.

(2) As to where should such control rest, and how should it be exercised.

So far the matter is simple, and there is no room for doubt or difference of opinion. But then the question arises, where should such control, immediate and mediate, rest, and how should it be exercised. To this question the answer is not easy, and it has given rise to much difference of opinion. It will be convenient to begin with schools which form the primary working units of our Education system.

One simple answer to the question of control in the case of a school would be that immediate control should rest with the head master. That answer is correct so far as the daily routine work of the school is concerned, but it is not a complete answer to the question, as there are many other matters connected with a school besides its daily routine work.

The founders of a school, whether they are the donors or merely the organizers of its funds, and whether they are private individuals or a public body, are the persons primarily entitled to control its working. They may delegate their power to others, and the matter for consideration is, who are the persons to whom their power of control ought properly to be delegated. The parties interested are, in the first place the students for whose benefit the school exists, the teachers from whom that benefit is to be derived, the founders through whose exertion the school came into existence, and the community whose future welfare depends upon the training which the rising generation may receive. But the students by reason of immature age are unable to understand their real interest and to select their proper representatives, and they must be represented by their guardians who are members of the local public. The founders of the school also in the majority of cases belong to the local public. So that practically the parties who ought to be represented on the governing body of a school are the teachers and the local public. The representation of the teachers is easy to secure by a rule requiring the teaching staff to choose two or three persons from amongst themselves to represent them. The proper representation of the local public must depend upon the good sense and discrimination of the founders of the school and of its succeeding managing committees, in selecting fit persons to serve on the managing committee. There is however, one natural guarantee for selection of proper persons, namely, that if such selection is not made, the school will cease to attract students.

If the difficult question in regard to immediate control is, how to secure adequate representation of all interests in the governing body, the difficulty in regard to mediate control is to determine with whom such control should rest.

Control of Primary Education.

As regards Primary Education, mediate or ultimate control ought to rest with the Government which will have to supply the funds for the maintenance of primary schools. And even when such funds are supplied by private liberality, the Government which is responsible for preservation of peace and order, ought to have the right of negative control at least, that is the right to prevent the imparting of such Education as may incite people to anarchy and disorder.

Control of Secondary Education.

As regards Secondary Education, there are two conflicting opinions. Some contend that the mediate control of all Secondary Schools should rest with Government, while others urge that it should rest with the Universities, the Government having only the ultimate right of negative control as mentioned in the preceding paragraph, and a partial right of positive control only over schools maintained by its funds. As the question is one of great importance, and as the future progress of Education will depend in a great measure upon its determination, let us examine closely the reasons by which the two conflicting views are sought to be supported.

The reasons urged, as far as I have been able to gather them, in support of the view that the mediate control over Secondary Schools should rest with the Government and not with the Universities, are the following :—

In the *first* place, it is said that the connection of Secondary Schools with Universities is not a necessary one but is casual only, resting upon the mere circumstance of their sending up students to the Matriculation Examination of the Universities. But as only a small number of those students really intend to enter University, while the majority of them either close their student life altogether after passing that examination, or continue their further study in institutions such as Medical, Engineering, or Technical Schools, wholly unconnected with any University, these huge Matriculaton Examinations which are a needlessly embarrassing burden on Universities, should be abolished, and then there will be no real connection between them and the Schools.

In the *second* place, it is urged that the Universities have no machinery for inspection and supervision of the Schools, and that that work is now done only nominally by the Universities, but really by the Government Education Department through Inspectors and Assistant Inspectors of Schools.

Thirdly, it is said that the Matriculation Examination has failed in its object of testing the fitness of students to enter the University, when Colleges complain that they are unfit to follow the lectures of professors. So that the Matriculation Examination is not only a heavy but is a useless burden on Universities, while it proves embarrassing to Schools by compelling them to maintain a uniform curriculum fixed by the Universities and practically depriving them of the power of adjusting their courses of study to suit the requirements of students who do not intend to enter the University. The abolition of that huge Matriculation Examination, and the substitution, on the one hand, of a School Final Examination to test the completion of a student's Secondary or School Education, and on the other hand, of a smaller and more suitable Matriculation Examination or College Entrance Examination to test the fitness of a student to enter College, will therefore be for the benefit of educational institutions and students alike.

And *fourthly* and lastly, it is intimated, though not stated as explicitly as the other reasons are, that the control of the University is not likely to be as effective as that of the Government Education Department, in keeping Secondary Schools and their students out of the reach of improper and injurious influences.

To these objections to the present system, those who are in favour of that system, and I should add that I am one of them, return the following answers.

In the *first* place they say it is a mistake to suppose that the connection between Secondary Schools and Universities is a merely casual one. The real foundation for all Education is laid in the former, and it is only the superstructure that is raised by the latter; and though in the end the superstructure is what appears prominently in view, while tne foundation remains hidden below, yet the foundation forms the necessary support of the superstructure, and the connection between the two is a necessary one. To leave the University to select its students from amongst those trained by Schools working unconnected with it, will be something like leaving the engineer or builder to go about probing the ground to find out fit firm site whereon to erect his intended edifice at once, without laying a proper foundation for it such as he requires under his own supervision. The Matriculation Examination, that is, the examination for testing the fitness of students to enter the University, must be controlled by the University, and the curriculum for that examination must be fixed by the University, and Schools which train students for that examination must partially at least be under the control of the University. It does not matter much if all the students who pass the Matriculation Examination do not enter the University. Many, perhaps the majority, do; and as for the rest, neither they, nor the institutions that bring them up, are any the worse for that.

It is said that this latter class of students, could have been better prepared for Medical, Engineering, or Technical Schools which they eventually enter, if they had not gone up for the Matriculation Examination, and if the schools which taught them had not been controlled by the University, and had been free to prepare them for their ultimate destination. But this argument is not sound. It is based upon the erroneous assumption that those students who after passing the Matriculation Examination do not enter the University, intended not to do so when preparing for that examination, and read for it and appeared at it only because there was no other course of study to pursue, and no other School Final Examination to appear at. That however is not the fact. In the great majority of cases, those who do not enter the University, did intend originally to do so, and are eventually obliged to give up that intention only because their circumstances do not permit them to carry it out, and not unfrequently because they cannot obtain admission into any College affiliated to the University.

Then again, because a school is preparing students for the Matriculation Examination, that is no reason why, if its resources permit, it should not have classes for preparing students specially for Engineering or Technical Education. Moreover, preparation for the Matriculation Examination is no bad preparation for entering a Medical or an Engineering School or even a Technical School.

Considering the vast population of the country, the number of students who appear at the Matriculation Examination and seek to enter the University, is by no means disproportionately large. And if the number is too large for one University, that objection will soon be removed by the establishment of the Universities of Dacca and Patna.

In the *second* place, the supporters of the present system say that though the Universities have no regularly organized machinery for inspection of schools, and they have to get the work of inspection done with the help of Government Inspectors of Schools, yet they associate some one or more members of their Senate with those Inspectors, so that, the joint inspection of Schools becomes much more efficacious than the inspection by the Education Department.

In answer to the *third* objection against the controlling of Schools by the Universities, the supporters of the present system say that granting for argument's sake that the Matriculation Examination through which Universities control Schools, has failed to prove a sufficient test of the fitness of students to enter College, that may be a reason for modifying the standard of the Matriculation Examination, but is no good reason for substituting for it a School Final Examination. If the University of which the Director of Public Instruction, and leading Inspectors of Schools and Principals and Professors of Colleges are prominent members, cannot with their combined assistance along with the assistance of others, prescribe proper courses of study and provide proper methods of examination, what guarantee is there that the Director of Public Instruction with the aid of his Inspectors of Schools will be able to make the proposed School Final Examination a better test of fitness? And if Colleges are left to hold there own entrance examination there will be no uniformity in the standard of fitness and the result will be most unsatisfactory.

The supporters of the present system further urge that the objection, if well founded, that the Matriculation Examination has failed to prove a sufficient test of the student's knowledge of English, may be easily removed by recommending students to read more suitable books than Macaulay's Lays of Ancient Rome and Kipling's Jungle Book and other similar books, which though they may teach a great deal, do not help a foreigner much to learn English.

In answer to the last objection that the University cannot as effectually prevent Schools from falling under or exercising improper influence as the Government Education Department can, it is urged that the assumption is not well founded on fact.

And it is pointed out that in one notable instance in which a University declined to give effect to a recommendation of a Local Government to disqualify a School for certain purposes, the action of the University met with the approval of the Supreme Government.

After a careful consideration of the reasons on both sides, I think the correct conclusion to be arrived at is, that while the immediate control of Secondary Schools should remain with their governing bodies (or the Education Department in the case of Government Schools) and the ultimate control of them and indeed of all educational institutions must rest with the Government, the intermediate control of all Secondary Schools should as heretofore rest with the Universities.

The main objection against the present system of control is that School Education is outside the Scope of Universities, and the placing of Secondary Schools under the control of Universities is prejudicial to the interests of both, as it throws on the one hand, an unnecessary burden on the latter, and on the other hand the latter are ill provided to exercise adequate and wholesome control over the former. This objection, as has been pointed out above is (speaking with all deference) based on a narrow and mistaken view. In the first place, the line drawn between School Education and College or University Education is an artificial and a conventional one. It may be helpful by way of division of labour, but division of labour must be regulated by union of design planned by some common superior agency. If you dissociate Secondary Schools altogether from Universities, where will you have this common superior agency that will plan your system of Education as a whole, whereof School Education and College Education are only two successive but closely connected parts? At present the Universities while working directly or indirectly through themselves or their affiliated Colleges for the latter part, regulate the former which is worked out by its recognized Schools. The only possible reasonable objection to this is that it throws a heavy burden on Universities. But that is a legitimate and an unavoidable burden which the Universities should bear, if the system of General Education in its different stages is to be worked out as a connected whole; and the proper reform will be to help the University with men and money to do the work, and not to help it out of a part of its field of work altogether by introducing a different agency. Those accustomed by the surroundings in which they are brought up to speak and think of School Education and University Education as two totally distinct things, may find it difficult at first sight to understand how one can reasonably talk of treating the two as connected and capable of being worked out by a common agency. To them I would say with all due deference, that those whose freedom of thought in this matter is not hampered by the tyranny of habit, find it difficult quite the other way, namely, to understand how things so closely connected can be regarded as so radically distinct and as unworkable by a common agency. The tenacity with which even cultured minds cling to traditional beliefs, is well illustrated in the story of the conservative lawyer who could not think it possible even for Parliament by statute law to validate a contingent remainder without a supporting estate.

Secondary or School Education must be the foundation for higher or University Education, and the University must therefore be the proper authority to see that the foundation is well and truly laid.

Then there is one clear advantage in the present system which places Secondary Schools under the mediate control of Universities. In this system the University holds one public examination, namely, the Matriculation Examination which serves as a test at once of the completion of a student's school career and of his fitness to enter the University, whereas the proposal to place Secondary Schools under the Education Department and to substitute the School Final Examination for the Matriculation Examination, will necessitate the institution of another examination by the University to test a student's fitness to enter College, and thus there will have to be held two public examinations in place of one, involving much needless expenditure of time, energy, and money.

It might be said that the School Final Examination may be accepted by the University as a test not only of a student's completion of School Education but also of his fitness to enter College; but if an examination held by the Education Department following a course of instruction given by Schools, over which examination and course of instruction the University has no control, can be accepted by the University as a sufficient test, why may not the Matriculation Examination held by the Uuiversity of which officers of the Education Department are prominent members, after a course of instruction given by the Schools themselves, be accepted not only as a test of fitness for receiving higher Education, but also as a test of completion of School Education and of fitness for certain lower grades of Government Service? If the present Matriculation standard is considered insufficient for any particular purpose, the proper course is to modify it in the necessary direction, and not to abolish it altogether.

Moreover, there are two or three special reasons, why in this country Secondary Schools should be placed under University control.

In the first place, University Education in India is imparted through the medium, not of the student's vernacular but of a difficult foreign language, the earlier steps for learning which must be taken during the period of School Education. It is but reasonable, therefore, that the Universities should regulate the teaching of English in Secondary Schools so as to qualify students for receiving University Education.

In the second place, our Universities are composed of Indian aud European members who have co-ordinate authority, while in the Government Education Department, Indian members occupy only a subordinate position, so that the control exercised by the University is likely to be better adapted to Indian conditions and to be more regardful of Indian requirements than the control of the Education Department.

The chief merit (in the eyes of certain narrow minded and short sighted reformers the chief defect) of the Universities is that their constitution is leavened by a large admixture of the popular element composed not merely of Indians but of Anglo-Indians as well, which serves to soften the severity of action of the official element, so that in the end the course of action generally taken is the right middle course lying between the extremes of leniency and stringency.

That is the reason why the public in this country are so anxious to have the jurisdiction of Universities extended instead of being curtailed, just as, (to compare two dissimilar things with a marked point of similitude) the public are anxious for the maintenance in all its integrity, of the jurisdiction of the High Courts which with their inherited strong instincts of British justice help to moderate any undue rigour of the Anglo-Indian Executive.

I may here refer to one recent instance shewing how the University moderates the rigour of official attitude.

That was an instance in which the Syndicate of the Calcutta University recommended to the Senate that certain students who owing to illness or other just cause had failed to attend the requisite 75 per cent of the lectures in certain subjects, might be admitted to their examinations as non-collegiate students. On the recommendation being duly placed before the Senate for acceptance, a learned member of the Senate who is also a prominent member of the Government Education Department, opposed the acceptance of the recommendation on this among other grounds, namely, that a student who was unable to attend lectures owing to illness, must be deemed to have been unfit to study his subjects and to prepare himself for his examination, forgetting that one may not be well enough to be able to come to the lecture room to attend lectures and yet he may be able to study at home. The opposition failed, as it ought to have failed, before the Senate; but if the decision had rested with the Department to which the gentleman opposing the recommendation belonged, the decision would in all probability have been in his favour.

Let it not be thought that my saying all this implies any leaning on my part in favour of laxity or undue leniency. I yield to none in my desire to maintain strict discipline in every sphere of life, and especially in the educational field where character begins to form. As a Hindu, I deeply love and highly respect the old type of student life, a life of rigid discipline and austere asceticism. Only, I would insist upon discipline being self-imposed through the student's internal feeling of respect for it, and not enforced by external authority. It is true that in the early stages, discipline has to be enforced in order to accustom the neophyte to it, but it should be imposed with loving kindness and not with supercilious contempt. I need hardly point out that it is only when discipline is voluntarily submitted to, that it produces any real good, and that discipline enforced by mere severity of treatment, creates a revulsion of feeling not only against the trainer, but also against discipline itself.

Any proposed measure of educational reform which seeks to substitute for a controlling agency with a popular and moderating element an agency without such element, should, therefore, be strongly deprecated in the true interests of Education and discipline.

There is one other cogent reason why the mediate control of Secondary Schools should not be vested in the Government Education Department. There are at present in Bengal Proper over four hundred Secondary Schools recognized by the University. Of these, some have been founded and are maintained by Government, others receive aid from Government, while a third section have been founded and are maintained exclusively by private individuals or private bodies. Now while on the one hand there can be no reasonable objection to the first two classes of Schools being controlled by the University of which the Head of the Education Department and other members of that Department are prominent members, on the other hand the placing of the third class under the control of the Education Department cannot be considered equally free from objection, when it is remembered that cases involving conflict of interest between Government Schools and Schools under private management not unfreqnently arise. With all respect for an officer of the high position of a Director of Public Instruction, one may say, as I remarked in my Note of Dissent from the Report of the majority of the Indian Universities Commission (p. 80), that the Syndicate of the University of which he will always be a member, and which has other responsibe members associated with him, would be a better authority to determine any question than he alone can be.

The proposed change will therefore militate against the principles of Simplicity, Parsimony, and Justice, enunciated in the first Chapter.

The institution of the Entrance or Matriculation Examination and the placing of Secondary Schools under University control, have led to the rapid multiplication of that class of Schools, and the rapid dissemination of Secondary Education. Sir H. Maine in his Convocation speech of 1864 observed with pleasure, "The number of entrances has positively sextupled since the foundation of the University six years ago, which is a rate of growth seldom seen out of the tropics." And he added, "Knowing as I do how deeply the taste for University distinctions penetrates even in England, although there it has to compete with the almost infinitely varied and multiplied forms which English enterprise assumes, I think I could have foreseen that a society like the native society of Bengal—a society whose faults no less than its excellencies lie on the side of mental acuteness, and which from its composition and circumstances has comparatively few facilities for the exercise of activity—I could have foreseen that such a society could be stirred to its inmost depths by an institution which conferred visible and tangible rewards on the early and sometimes, it is to be feared, precocious display of intellectual ability." The rapid early rate of growth has, it is true, been moderated by time, but steady growth of Secondary Schools is still maintained under the fostering care of the Universities; and the reason of it has been well pointed out in the above passage of Sir H. Maine's speech. The Entrance or Matriculation Examination held by the Indian Uuiversities is so largely attended by Indian youths, not only because it is a test of completion of School Education and a passport to the lower grades of Government service, but also because it enables them to gratify their honest ambition (which has so few facilities for gratification) by the attainment of the modest rank of undergraduates.

The placing of High Schools under the control of the

Education Department and the substitution of the School Final for the Matriculation Examination will, therefore, operate as a serious check on the further progress of Secondary Education. The proposed change should not therefore be introduced unless such a check is deemed desirable. It is apprehended in certain quarters that a check of this sort is really intended. I cannot readily persuade myself to believe that an enlightened Government administered by statesmen and scholars can seriously intend to adopt such retrograde policy. It is true that the number of young men receiving General Secondary Education is far in excess of those that can find employment, and that General Education now urgently requires to be supplemented by Technical Education, to enable our young men to earn their livelihood. But the remedy lies in opening new fields of work, and not in closing the only field now open. Let easily accessible institutions be opened for imparting Technical Education in its different branches, and they will attract large numbers of those who now seek General Education, and thus remove the congestion that is complained of.

Upon all these considerations, I would submit, with all the earnestness I am capable of, that the existing system of having Secondary Schools under the control of the Universities and of having the completion of Secondary Education tested by the Matriculation Examination, should be maintained with any suitable changes in the Matriculation standard that may be deemed necessary, and with ample provision for Technical Education to relieve the University from its present congestion.

Control of Higher Education.

As regards Higher Education, while immediate control should rest with Government in the case of Government Colleges, and with their governing bodies as constituted by their founders in the case of private Colleges, mediate control should rest with the University as regards all Colleges of both classes affiliated to it. So far the matter is quite simple. But there is one class of Colleges somewhat anomalous, regarding which a difficulty may arise, namely, Colleges established and maintained by the Uuiversities themselves. If the governing body of such a College has (as it may have) the Vice-Chancellor for its *ex-officio* President, and the Director of Public Instruction as an *ex-officio* member, then, as both of them are also *ex-officio* members of the Syndicate, the governing body and the body exercising mediate control over it will have two very influential members in common, and the mediate control that is to be exercised by the latter, will either be nominal only or will give rise to embarrassing conflicts. The difficulty may to some extent be avoided by a rule excluding the Vice-Chancellor from membership of the governing body of any University College. But one may go further and doubt the propriety of the University establishing any College which is of rank and rights co-ordinate with those of ordinary affiliated Colleges, and which works in competition with them. For such competition will often be an unequal competition, and an ordinary affiliated College will often have to work at a disadvantage in comparison with a University College. The foregoing remarks will not apply, for obvious reasons, where as in the case of the University of Cambridge, the office of Vice-Chancellor is elective, and the election is from among the heads of affiliated Colleges.

The question raised above is part of a larger question, namely, What is the true meaning of a Teaching University?—a question which will be considered in its proper place under the fifth head of my discourse, that is, Methods of Imparting Education. Here it will be enough to say that, in the *first* place a Teaching University in the narrow sense of the term, is, a University teaching directly through its professors, and is no more than a large College, or a federation of a few Colleges in a limited area; and its sphere of usefulness is limited by its local extent. And in the *second* place, a Teaching University in the wider sense of the term, that is a University of the type of the Calcutta University, is not a mere examining body, but is an instrument of teaching as well, and it regulates and controls its teaching not only through its professors by imparting higher instruction, but also through the courses of study it prescribes for its affiliated Colleges, and the control it exercises over them through its inspecting agency and its examinations. Opinion is divided as to which of the two is the better type. But in any view, it is not desirable that a University should establish a College for the teaching of undergraduates, though it may appoint lecturers for such purpose, and that it is not desirable also that the Vice-Chancellor should be a member of the governing body of any College established by the University.

Control of Professional Education.—The immediate control of Colleges imparting Professional Education should rest with their governing bodies as constituted by their founders, and their mediate control, where the Education they impart leads up to University degrees, should rest with the Universities to which they are affiliated. And the remarks made above regarding Colleges established by Universities are applicable quite as much to Colleges imparting Professional Education, as they are to Colleges for giving General Education.

Control of Technical Education.—Institutions imparting Technical Education should be controlled in a manner similar to that in which Colleges for Professional Education are controlled, with this difference, that as Technical Education does not generally lead up to any University degree,

Technical Schools and Colleges will seldom come under the mediate control of Universities. Mediate control in their case will rest either with associations of technical experts with which they may be connected, or with official experts in departments of Government which deal with their respective subjects.

Control over Universities.—State Control.—The last question for consideration under the head of Control of Education is, whether Universities should be subject to any higher controlling agency, and what should be the nature and scope of the ultimate control of the State over Education. Some are of opinion that a public body like a University should not be subject to any higher controlling authority, and that any control which Government may justly exercise over it, should be exercised through such Government officials and others whom it may appoint as members of the Senate. Others mantain that over and above the control exercised through its representatives on the Senate, the State should have an ultimate control over Universities, and indeed over all educational institutions, a control which should, however, be exercised sparingly and cautiously. With proper limitations the latter view is the correct one.

In relation to Education, the State stands in two distinct capacities, one as the proprietor of schools and colleges founded and maintained by it, and the other as the preserver of peace and promoter of prosperity in the realm, bound to see that no Education is imparted which is injurious to peace and prosperity. In the former capacity, the only control it can claim to exercise is what can be exercised through its official representatives as members of the Senate, while in its latter capacity, it may not only exercise control through fit and proper persons appointed as members of the Senate to represent different public interests, but also over and above that, it may control the action of the Senate by its paramount power of vetoing decisions of the Senate. The existence of such power is necessary as an ultimate safeguard against any case of a wrong decision of the Senate proving injurious to peace and order. From the nature of things, such cases must be extremely rare, and the exercise of such power must consequently be of rare occurrence. But there are two important limitations by which the exercise of the power should be governed. In the *first* place, the power should be exercised most sparingly and only in very extreme cases. It should produce its salutary effect more by the moral influence of its potential existence than by the natural consequences of its actual exercise. And in the *second* place, it should be exercised only by the highest functionaries of the State, that is, only by the heads of the Supreme and Local Governments. Paramount as is the importance of the existence of this power of ultimate control in the Government in the interests of peace and order in cases of extreme necessity, it is of no less importance in the interests of Education that the acts and decisions of a dignified body like the Senate of a University should be allowed to remain intact and unimpeachable from without as far as possible. And with the limitations suggested above, the ultimate power of Government control will leave the dignity of the Senate practically unimpaired.

CHAPTER IV.

ORGANIZATION OF A SYSTEM OF EDUCATION.

I come now to the fourth head of my discourse, namely, the Organization of a System of Education.

I have already considered what the different parts of a System of Education should be, under the head of Different Kinds of Education, and have said that they are,

I. Physical Education,

II. Intellectual Education including

(1) General Education,

(2) Professional Education and

(3) Technical Education,

III. Moral Education,

IV. Religious Education,

with their subdivisions.

I. Physical Education.

I shall here make only two suggestions about Physical Education. In the *first* place, Physical Education should not be confined to mere training in the practice of athletics, but should iuclude also teaching of the principles of Hygiene and Sanitation. That is the only way in which Education may, as our Government desires it should, help sanitary improvement, and that is the only way to make our students physically fit for athletics. And in the *second* place, I say with some hesitation, but with great hope of being heard with attention, that violent physical exercise, though it may be suited to a cooler climate, is altogether unsuitable under the tropical sun, and when resorted to under the overpowering and unhealthy stimulus of competition for prize, it is, except for the peculiarly gifted few, positively injurious to health instead of being conducive to it. In many instances, young men in this country have permanently ruined their health by taking too much to athletic games and sports. Moreover, many among those who are ready to exhibit their agility and strength in the cricket or foot-ball field in the expectation of prizes or under the stimulus of applause, will be found slow to work or walk in sun or rain in the dreary cheerless walks of daily life. Then again, it is a curious sight to see, that to witness the performances of not more than fifty young men, more than five thousand men, young and old, throng round and remain staying for hours on damp soil or under a burning sun, unmindful of actual present discomfort and risk of future illness. It seems that the matter is becoming one of fashion. Physical exercise should be less exciting, less violent, more capable of being joined in, instead of being merely witnessed, by large numbers, more conducive to ordinary health, and better calculated to make young men enduring, hardy, and diligent in doing ordinary work.

II. Intellectual Education.

(1) *General Education.—Primary Education.*

I begin with General Education, that is, the first head of Intellectual Education, and shall consider first its first subdivision, Primary Education.

I have said before that though at one time I was, on further reflection I no longer am, in favour of compulsory Primary Education, as the evils of a compulsory system of Primary Education outweigh its benefits. But at the same time I am decidedly in favour of offering facilities for Primary Education by the establishment of well conducted Primary Schools at convenient distances, and of offering encouragement to people to receive Primary Education, by giving those who send their boys to Primary Schools, and also those who have finished their Primary Education and have attained majority, the priviledge of voting at municipal and other similar elections, irrespective of their property qualifications.

The points for consideration here are—

(1) What should be the duration of the Primary course of study, when should it begin, and when should it end?

(2) What subjects should be included in the course?

(3) What should the extent of each subject be? and

(4) What should be the nature of the text-books?

The period of study for the Primary stage should be, not less then two and not more then three years, and the minimum age for admission to a Primary School should be five years, and the maximum age, eight years, with a view to prevent very little boys and very big boys reading together in one and the same class.

The Primary course of study should be easy, as otherwise it would deter many from taking it up.

The course should include Reading, Writing and Arithmetic, the three time-honoured R's, and a little science to meet the requirements of modern times. As regards reading and writing, that is, language, the question arises whether there should be only one language, the student's vernacular, or whether English should be included as well. It is said, and I think rightly, that a purely vernacular Education is not very popular. And some even go the length of wrongly inferring therefrom that people in this country do not care for their vernacular. The truth is that English is valued by people generally as the language of our rulers and the medium of communication with them, and also as a sort of *Lingua Franca* for all India; and it is valued by educated people as furnishing a key to unlock the treasures of the world's thought in all ages and countries. In my opinion English should be included in the Primary course, which will thus consist of

1. The student's vernacular, Bengali,
(I speak here only of Bengal),
2. English,
3. Arithmetic, and
4 Science, that is, a few facts of the material world methodically arranged.

Turning now to the extent of subjects, I think Bengali should include simple Prose and simple Poetry written in a style neither too Sanskritized nor too colloquial and provincial. Some educationists think that the language of the Primary course Reading Lessons should be colloquial and provincial so that the student may be spared the trouble of learning the polished language of the learned. But that is mistaken kindness, which again may be misunderstood as deep policy. We are all anxious to raise the depressed classes and soften the rigour of caste distinctions, except where they are interwoven with religion, and one of the best solvents of the rigidity of caste is Education. But Education will not obtain for the lower castes admission into genteel society unless it gives their language a little polish. Nor, considering the simplicity of the Bengali of genteel society, will it cost the lower classes much real labour to learn it. So that while the mistaken tenderness which induces educationists to advocate the retention of provincial colloquialisms in the language of books for the Primary course is on the one hand unnecessary, and injurious to the interests of those whom it is intended to serve, on the other hand it is liable to be misconstrued as being the out-come of a desire to prevent the union of the people of different districts through unity of language.

While speaking of national unity through unity of language, I may here make a passing reference to a connected question, namely, whether it is possible to have a common script for all India. All the Indian vernaculars derived from Sanskrit (and they form the great majority of the leading vernaculars) have a common alphabet, and it is only the characters that are different. And as Nagari characters are used in almost all these vernaculars except Bengali and Uriya, Mr. Sarada Charan Mitra started the idea that if Nagari characters are adopted in Bengal and Orissa, we may have a coonmm script for all India. He has been working at it steadily, but his project has not made much progress. Many years ago, before Mr. Mitra's scheme was started, I prevailed upon my colleagues in the Syndicate of the Calcutta University to pass a resolution requiring candidates for examination to write Sanskrit in Devanagari characters. And I wrote a small pamphlet to show that the resolution involved no hardship on Bengali candidates by pointing out the evident similarity of Devanagari characters with Bengali characters. But notwithstanding all that, the modest and reasonable resolution of the Syndicate was rescinded shortly after its adoption. So I am not very hopeful about Mr. Sarada Charan Mitra's proposal being adopted. And as far as Bengali characters are concerned, we are bound to admit that they are much simpler than Nagari characters and are not likely to be easily replaced by the latter.

I would here suggest only one improvement in writing and printing Bengali, which I think may be found acceptable, namely, the replacing of compound consonants or at least such of them as wholly differ in form from their components, by their components placed in close juxta position, one after the other, or if that interferes with economy of space, one below the other in reduced size, without any change of shape in either. In the existing method of writing and printing, compound consonants differ much in shape from their components, so that the learner has to learn many new forms of compound letters, a knowledge of the forms of the components not being sufficient. This throws an unnecessary difficulty in the way of the learner and involves waste of energy which may easily be prevented by adopting the above suggestion.

I have one important suggestion to make with regard to the prose and poetical pieces of which the Primary Reading Book should be composed. No piece, or better still, no sentence, should contain more than twenty five per cent of words that are likely to be new to the learner. For if a new lesson or a new sentence contains a large proportion of unknown words, the pain involved in the labour of learning them will outweigh the pleasure derived from learning what is new. The rule I suggest is no doubt a very artificial one; but it need not be literally followed. It will be enough if it be observed in spirit. It may be difficult to select pieces that fulfil the requirements of the rule. But with some care selections may be made which substantially comply with the requirements to the rule.

Turning now from the form to the matter of the prose and poetical pieces to be selected, I think we should try to economize time, money, and energy, by selecting the pieces so that they may be suitable for teaching not only reading and writing, that is language, but also in teaching simple facts of Nature which are of daily occurrence, simple facts of the history of India, lessons from the lives of men with whose names the learner is familiar, and elementary truths of morality. And the different pieces should be arranged after some method and not given at random.

The course in Arithmetic should include the Four Fundamental Operations simple and compound, Vulgar Fractions, and the Rule of Three treated according to the Unitary method. A knowledge of principles should be required in addition to a mere knowledge of the rules of operation. The *Subhankari* method should not be included, as it is not of general application, its use being confined to cases in which the units of money are the rupee and its old sub-divisions, the units of weight, the maund and its subdivisions, and the units of land measure, the bigha and its subdivisions.

The course in Science is difficult to define with precision except by prescribing a text book. All that can be said in general terms is, that the course should consist of a methodical statement of the chief simple facts of the mineral, vegetable, and animal kingdoms, including under the first mentioned head some account of the earth, water, and air, of shape, size and weight of bodies, of sound, light, heat and electricity, and of the phenomena of day and night, sunshine and rain and the seasons; and including under the two latter heads, some account of growth and decay, and life and death. Lastly, the Science course should include a little of drawing and clay moulding.

The course in English should comprise reading and writing just so far as is included in an alphabetical primer.

The text-books for the Primary Course require great care in their preparation. It entails great labour in writing an elementary text-book on any subject for beginners; but the labour spent by the author in writing a good text book is amply repaid by the saving it effects in the labour of the learner; and it is only those who value repayment in that way, and not by pecuniary remuneration, that are really fit to undertake the work.

The first question for consideration here is, whether elementary text-books should be prepared by small committees of experts appointed by Government or any other public body, or whether they should be selected from among the books available in the market. Each of the two methods has its advantages and disadvantages. The advantage of the first method is, that we have the combined wisdom of several competent persons brought to bear upon the work, and we may expect that the book will be in greater conformity with our requirements than it would be if it was written by any irresponsible person. Its disadvantages are those of monopoly—the writers feeling secure about their remuneration, and (if, they do not care for pecuniary gain) secure also about the success of their labour by the adoption of their book, have no inducement to exertion except what arises from a sense of duty; and then again there will be an utter absence of inducement to the literary public to produce good text-books. The advantages of the second method are just the opposite of the disadvantages of the first, each author exerting his best for the success of his books, and the entire literary public having an inducement to compete. Its disadvantages are, that each author works for himself without having the benefit of the wisdom of any of his rivals, and there is less likelihood of this book being in exact conformity with our requirements than there is in the first method: moreover, the best authors may not enter the field of competition; and as only one book is to be selected, the books rejected will find no market, and thus there will be great waste of energy and money of the literary public taken as a whole.

Considering the advantages and disadvantages of the two methods, I think the balance of advantage is in favour of the latter; and its dis advantages may be minimized, (1) by publishing a concise but detailed syllabus of our requirements, (2) by issuing suitable invitations to authors without making any promise and reserving freedom of selection, and (3) by allowing proof copies only to be submitted to the Board or Committee appointed to make the selection. As the text-books for the Primary standard will be short, they may, without inconvenience, be kept in type, and authors may be found agreeable to comply with the last condition, so that eventually, only the book selected may be printed and published, and much waste of money may be prevented.

There is only one other point that remains to be noticed in connection with the Primary Course. Some educationists are of opinion that the Primary Course should be of two sorts:—one for those who want to pass on to the Secondary Course, and the other for those who want to pass off to a Technical Course of instruction, or want to stop in their educational career altogether. And it is said that the Primary Course ought to be a little longer and fuller for the latter two classes of students, to give their education a better finish, and to initiate them in subjects allied to Technical Education, such as those which train the hands and eyes. I have already given my reason for making the Primary Course simple and short, namely, that if we make it difficult or long, it will deter many from coming to receive Primary Education; and that reason applies with greater force to the case of those for whom it is sought to be made fuller and longer than to the case of others. As for training of the hands and eyes, there is no reason why it should not form part of the Primary Course for all students, whatever their subsequent career may be. My strongest reason against having a double course is that it introduces a needless complication and violates the Principle of Simplicity.

Secondary Education.—I come now to the next head, Secondary Education, and the points requiring considerations are,

(1) What should be the duration of the Secondary Course of study, and when should it begin and when should it end?

(2) What subjects should the Secondary Course include? Should there be any alternative optional subjects?

(3) What should the extent of subjects be? and

(4) What should be the nature of the text-books?

The first three points are connected with one another, and the consideration of the first point will to some extent involve the consideration of the second and the third.

The duration of the course will evidently depend upon the number and extent of the subjects to be included. It will depend also upon the age of the student at which the course is begun, as a student of comparatively mature age will be able to finish it sooner than one of younger years.

It may be said that as we have fixed the duration and extreme age limits for the Primary Course, and as the Secondary Course is to begin just where the Primary Course ends, the age limits for the Secondary Course have been necessarily fixed, and that these limits should be not lower than the completion of the seventh year and not higher than the completion of the eleventh. That however will be true only for those cases in which students go through their Primary Course in a public school; and those who do not go to School in the Primary stage, may begin and end their Primary Education earlier or later. Moreover a student may not join a Secondary School at the beginning of his Secondary Course, but may come to school after studying that course for any indefinite time at home. But those are exceptional cases, and we may take the eighth year as the ordinary average lower limit of age for the commencement of Secondary Education. Nor will it be unreasonable to fix the twelfth year as the year ordinary higher limit. They are to be taken however only as rough limits, and not as exact limits to be strictly observed for purposes of admission to Secondary Schools.

Taking the eighth year to be the ordinary age limit for admission to a Secondary School, and accepting the commencement of the sixteenth year, fixed by the wisdom of Indian sages as the attainment of majority, to be the ordinary lower age limit for entering the University, we get eight years as the duration of the Secondary stage of Education, and that does not differ materially from the average period of a student's stay at school now. The question then arises whether this period is sufficient to enable a student of average intelligence to complete his Secondary Education, having regard to the number and extent of the subjects which the Secondary Course should include, and to qnalify himself for receiving Collegiate Education.

The line separating the School course from the Collegiate is to some extent at any rate a conventional and a changing one. The nature of the subject may in some cases help us in determining whether its proper place is in the one course or in the other, but that is not true of all subjects, nor has physiological psychology definitely determined yet, at what age the human brain becomes fit to learn what particular subject. Then again, with the progress of society and the advancement of knowledge, the extent of knowledge necessary to be acquired in the Secondary stage must go on increasing, in order to enable the student to begin the higher course at a sufficiently advanced stage so that he may keep pace with the onward march of time. Specialization in particular subjects or particular branches of one and the same subject, is one of the modes now adopted to meet the altered situation, but that does not always solve the difficulty satisfactorily. Then again, in the self-adjusting economy of Nature, with the rise in the upper level of knowledge in any society, the lower level also rises though at a slower rate imperceptibly, and the student commences his Education with a starting stock of knowledge, picked up in social intercourse without conscious effort, which is much in excess of what students in less advanced stages of society have to begin with. So that we need not make any violent spasmodic effort to raise the standard of Secondary Education. We may, therefore, for the present take eight years as sufficient for the completion of Secondary Education for ordinary students.

The age limit for commencement of Secondary Education mentioned above, is, as I have said, only a rough limit; and no strict age limit is, as far as I am aware, prescribed anywhere for that purpose. But a strict age limit has now been prescribed by our Universities for the commencement of Collegiate Education. The Regulations of the Calcutta University (See Chap. XXX. Para 3.) prohibit the admission of any candidate to the Matriculation Examination unless he has completed the age of sixteen years. There has been considerable fluctuation of opinion on the point. When the Calcutta University was established more than half a century ago, the rule was laid down that no candidate should be admitted to the Entrance Examination unless he had com pleted the age of sixteen years. That rule remained in force for some time, but it was then abrogated, and for many years there was no age limit for the Entrance Examination in any Indian University except the University of Allahabad. In 1902 the question came up for consideration before the Indian Universities Commission, which recommended the minimum limit of age as fifteen years, mainly for the reasons, namely, *first* that precocious mental progress was injurious to physical growth, and *second* that below the age of fifteen a student was unfit for collegiate life under the hostel system. I regret very much that I did not record in my Note of Dissent my disagreement with this recommendation in the Report of the Commission. But if the Universities Commission recommended fifteen years as the limit, the Calcutta University has raised it higher and fixed it at sixteen. And subsequent experience has shown that the operation of the age limit rule has been attended with much inconvenience and hardship.

Head masters of schools have been troubled with numerous applications for correction of age as recorded in admission registers, on the ground of the age being given erroneously on insufficient information. Many of those applications have been supported by reliable evidence, and considered reasonable and Head masters have felt it their duty to forward them to the Syndicate for favourable consideration. And the Syndicate has had to hold a sort of *quasi* judicial inquiry resulting in many cases in favour of the applicants. Then again, many brilliant boys have had to be kept back from appearing at the Matriculation Examination, causing them no small discouragement. And in some instances in which candidates were provisionally admitted to the Examination pending inquiry into the question of age, it is said that they were, upon the result of the inquiry turning out against them, regarded as excluded from the Examanation although they were found to have passed the Examination.

This is a most undesirable state of things, and should not be allowed to continue, unless there are some more cogent reasons for having an age limit than those usually given. There is a natural guarantee against boys below a certain age appearing at the Matriculation Examination, for the simple reason that they will not be able to make themselves ready for it. As for those few who are able to qualify themselves for it earlier, there is not much danger of their health being injured by over work, as their superior intelligence will enable them to do their work without much labour. And parents or other guardians of boys may, as a rule, be safely trusted to prevent boys from injuring their health by over study. Again, granting that a student below the age of sixteen or fifteen is unfit for hostel life, that is no reason why they should not be allowed to enter a College. It is not absolutely necessary that every College student should live in a hostel. One may live with his guardian and attend College as a day scholar. If it is deemed desirable to keep a record of the age of every student, such record may be kept without excluding any student from any examination on the ground of his being under age. The age limit rule is not at all necessary to serve any useful purpose, and its operation is attended with considerable hardship and inconvenience. The rule should therefore be wholly abrogated. And if that is deemed to be going too far, then it ought at least to be modified and the limit fixed at fourteen or fifteen years.

My next point is, what subjects should the Secondary Course include? During the first three years of the Secondary stage, the course should consist of

(1) The student's Vernacular
(Prose and Poetry)
(2) English
(3) Arithmetic
(4) Science Lessons
(5) History (to be included in Vernacular Prose)
(6) Geography
(7) Drawing.

The number of subjects, though apparently seven, is really six, History being included in Vernacular Prose, or in other words, Vernacular Prose being a book on History. Some educationists take exception to this, and say that a text-book of History, however well-written, can never take the place of a literary work in prose. The objection is valid so far as higher literature, is concerned. There are in almost every language which has a literature, works of lasting literary value which not only teach language but also exercise the intellect and elevate the moral nature; and their place can never be filled by any historical text-book. When the student has advanced sufficiently to be able to understand and appreciate such literature, for him History and Literature must stand apart. And there is a further reason for that. For at that stage of the student's progress, History also will have its own special purpose to serve, which is not simply to present a narrative of events in elegant style but also to trace the course of the political, social, moral, and religious progress of the world on the one hand, and of its material and economic progress on the other. But in the earlier years of a student's progress in the Secondary Course, he can read neither Literature or History in that way, and for him the one may fill the place of the other, without any objection, and with evident advantage to him by enabling him to learn two subjects in one.

There is, therefore, during the first three years of the secondary stage, really only one subject added to the Primary Course, namely, Geography. And as it should be elementary Descriptive Geography, the addition will be no great burden. I need hardly point out that History and Geography are very important and at the same time very interesting subjects, and should be introduced early into the Secondary Course. They are our time chart and our space chart, and without some knowledge of them, we cannot fix our position in the world.

In the third year, considering the progress which the student has made in his Vernacular, a Grammar of his vernacular may with advantage be introduced, to initiate him in the study of the structure of language, and to serve as a stepping stone to the study of an allied classical language and of English Grammar in the next year.

From the fourth year, the Science Lessons may be dropped to make room for three additional subjects, namely, a Classical Language (Sanskrit for Hindus and Arabic or Persian for Mahomedans), English Grammar, and Algebra. A fourth subject, Geometry, should also be introduced as part of drawing, with demonstrations of simple propositions. And the place of Science Lessons may be regarded as filled up by advanced lessons in Geography treating of the phenomena of day and night, of the seasons, and of the flora and fauna of different countries.

Here two important questions arise, namely, *first*, whether it is necessary or desirable to have a Classical Language, and *second*, whether the subjects other than English should be taught in English or in the student's vernacular.

Regarding the importance of the two classical languages, Greek and Latin, as subjects of study, there has been considerable difference of opinion in the West, and it is not easy to say which side is right.

But I trust I shall not be charged with any undue partiality to the classical language of my country if I say that there is great difference between the educative value of Sanskrit and that of either Greek or Latin. No classical language has a grammar so elaborate and complete as Panini's immortal work. No classical language has an alphabet so scientific and so nearly perfect as Sanskrit. And no classical language has such a rich religious literature as Sanskrit. It is the study of Sanskrit that has given us the science of Comparative Philology. It is the study of Vedic literature that has given the world the science of Comparative Religion. Then again, there is no comparison between the practical importance of Sanskrit to Hindu India and that of Greek or Latin to Christian Europe. The religious books of the Hindu are written in Sanskrit, and his prayers and the formulae for his religious observances are all in Sanskrit. And lastly, his vernacular is much more closely connected with Sanskrit than is English, French or German with either Greek or Latin. No Hindu who is desirous of receiving liberal Education and of being called educated, should be wholly ignorant of Sanskrit. The same remarks apply more or less with regard to Arabic or Persian in the case of Mahomedans. I therefore do not feel any hesitation in saying that Sanskrit for Hindus and either Arabic or Persian for Mahomedans, should form a subject for the Secondary Course from the fourth year.

The second question is not equally easy to answer. Sentiment no doubt is in favour of making the student's vernacular the medium of imparting knowledge; and reason supports that sentiment to a great extent. A student will learn a subject sooner and more easily if taught in his vernacular than he can if he is taught through the medium of a foreign language, for the simple reason, that in the latter case he has to make a conscious effort in the first place to understand the language, and then to understand the subject. But then there are also strong reasons on the other side.

In the *first* place there are no good text-books, except a few in only some of the subjects; and those few cover only the elementary parts of their subjects.

In the *second* place, as the higher branches of all subjects will, for want of text-books, have to be taught in English, there will be no advantage, but on the contrary there will be a disadvantage, in teaching the elementary parts of the subjects in which there are text-books in the vernacular, because the student will in that case have to learn first the vernacular technical terms of those subjects and then again their English equivalents when he proceeds further.

And in the *third* place as the English language has to be learnt well for the purposes of daily business, official and non-official, in dealings with Englishmen, the learning of that language will be helped if, all subjects of study are taught in it.

The first reason can be easily met. There are Bengali text-books covering the elementary portions of several subjects. In Arithmetic there are many, and I have added one more to their number. In Algebra and Geometry according to modern method, I have contributed my mite ; the books in those two subjects give all that is required by the Calcutta University up to the standard for the Intermediate Examinations in Arts and Science. They may not be all that can be desired, but with better encouragement offered by the reading of those subjects in Bengali, other and better books will be forthcoming. In History and Geography, and Logic also, there are good books up to the standard for the Intermediate Examinations. And many more text-books in those and in other subjects, in Urdu and other vernaculars, may be expected to be written by competent authors if encouragement is received.

The Regulations of the Calcutta University framed under the presidency of the late Vice-Chancellor, Sir Ashutosh Mukherji, permit candidates to read History in Bengali and certain other vernaculars. And similar permission may be accorded in regard to Geography and Mathematics without causing any difficulty or inconvenience.

The second objection is so far valid, that for some years at least, the higher branches of every subject will have to be taught in English. But that does not necessitate the imparting of elementary knowledge such as is required for the Matriculation Examination, through the medium of the English language. And the inconvenience of the student's having to learn two sets of technical terms, will be more than compensated by the facility with which he will learn the subject in his vernacular, especially if the varnacular technical terms are suitably selected. The inconvenience may be obviated still further if the corresponding English technical terms are taught at the same time. Experience supports the view I take, for it is well-known that students who have learnt Arithmetic in Bengali for the Vernacular Scholarship Examination, prove better arithmeticians than those who learn it in English.

The third reason, though appearing cogent at first sight, is not really sound, as a little consideration will show. A student who learns his subjects through the medium of his vernacular, learns them in less time and with less labour than another who is taught those subjects in English ; and the spare time and energy which the former thus gets at his disposal, he can employ with advantage for the learning of English as a language, while the latter comes to his study of English as a language without that surplus time and energy, but on the contrary with a mind cramped by overwork in the study of his other subjects.

I would therefore submit that in the Secondary Course, that is up to the Matriculation Examination standard, subjects other than English should be taught in the student's vernacular wherever practicable.

The next point for consideration is whether there should be any alternative optional subjects in the Secondary Course. Some educationists are of opinion that though Sanskrit may be a desirable subject of study for those who intend to continue in a course of Liberal Education, it is of no use to those who are only preparing for Technical Education, and that the study of the elements of some branch of Physical Science in place of Sanskrit would be much better for them. That may be true for those who want to receive Technical Education as mere handicraftsmen, and they need not continue the study of the Secondary Course beyond the third year. But as regards those who intend to finish that Course before receiving Technical Education, their aim being a little more ambitious, the acquisition of a modicum of knowledge of a Classical Language will give them mental training which will fit them all the better for the higher and more intellectual kind of Technical Education which they aspire for.

In the interests of students, therefore, option in regard to subjects is unnecessary at this stage. And in the interests of schools, the allowing of option is most undesirable, as it introduces a complication which must interfere with efficiency.

At a higher stage of the Secondary Course, that is, in the Course for the Matriculation Examination, the Calcutta University allows a very large measure of option (see Regulations Ch. XXX para. 4), there being four compulsory subjects, and any two optional subjects out of the following five, namely.

(i) Additional Mathematics.

(ii) Additional extent of Classical Language.

(iii) History of India and Indian Administration.

(iv) Geography: general, mathematical and physical

(v) Elementary Mechanics.

So that a candidate has the choice of ten different combinations of subjects, that being the number of combinations of five things taken two at a time. This large extent of option is often embarrassing to schools in arranging their work and making their time tables, and not unoften embarrassing to students in whose interest it is allowed, and to their advisers, in making their choice. Let us pause for a moment and examine closely the reasons for and against this scheme.

The reasons which may be given in its favour are mainly two, namely, *first*, that this allowing of option makes the Matriculation course suit different tastes and varieties of mental capacity, and *second*, that it enables the student to prepare himself better for his after career. It may be said for instance, that some students have more liking and better capacity for the study of Language and History than for the study of Mathematics and Mechanics, while others have just the reverse, and the knowledge of the two last named subjects is better preparation than that of the two mentioned first, for those who intend to become engineers. That is true, but only partially true, true above certain limits, but not true below them. Within the moderate limits of the Matriculation standard, none of the important subjects of study, namely, Languages (Vernacular and Classical), History, Geography, and Mathematics, if properly taught, will be found repulsive to or beyond the grasp of, any ordinary sound mind. Even as regards Mathematics for which some students have a nervous dread, the cause of fear like that of fear of ghosts, is imaginary and not real. Then again, regard being had to the limit within which the options are allowed, the additional knowledge which the exercise of the option enables one to acquire, is for practical purposes of very little value to a student in his after career. Nor must we forget the fact, which is now matter of common knowledge, that what determines the decision of a student in the selection of his optional subjects is, not the consideration that any particular subject is specially suited to his taste or capacity, nor the consideration that it will be of use to him in his career in the remote future, but the simple consideration that it will help him in the near future in passing his examination; and the popularity or unpopularity of any subject in any year depends upon the simplicity or difficulty of the question paper in the subject in the preceding year.

The option allowed in the selection of subjects does not therefore practically lead to much good. But on the contrary it leads to much difficulty and many undesirable results. In the first place, it embarrasses schools in arranging their work and adjusting their time tables, and thus impairs their efficiency. In the second place, it often puzzles students and their advisers in the selection of their subjects. In the third place, it makes it possible for a candidate to become an undergraduate without knowing any thing of History and Geography. It may be said that although those two subjects are not compulsory for the Matriculation Examination, that does not prevent a student's reading them in the earlier years of the Secondary Course. But it is well known that except a small number of students who have special liking for those two subjects, the rest read them in a most half-hearted way, in the lower classes, because they think they will not have to read them for their final examination in the Secondary Course. One of these two subjects, namely, Geography, for the purpose of being raised to the rank of an independent subject, has got its extent and scope increased a little too much for the capacity of Matriculation candidates by the inclusion of Mathematical and Physical Geography; and only a very small number of schools is authorized to teach it, the rest being considered unfit to do so by reason of want of apparatus and appliances. Elementary Mechanics is required by the University Regulations to be treated mainly experimentally. Such treatment may be a useful supplement to, but can never be a good substitute for, intelligent study of the subject, which requires a little more knowledge of Mathematics than what the Matriculation candidate possesses. For want of such knowledge, the subject can only be studied mechanically to serve the purposes of an artistan, but can hardly be studied as a branch of liberal Education.

Speaking with all due deference, one feels bound to say that the scheme of studies for the Matriculation Examination of the Calcutta University, both as regards the subjects and their extent, is not a well-considered one, and requires to be thoroughly recast.

I would suggest that there should be no optional subject in the course of study up to the Matriculation standard, and that from the fifth year to the end that is the eighth year of the Secondary Course, the following should be the subjects of study, namely,

1. English (a full subject).
2. The student's Vernacular (a half subject).
3. A Classical Language (a full subject).
4. History and Elementary Geography (forming one complete full subject).
5. Mathematics (including Arithmetic, Algebra, and Geometry, and forming a full subject).
6. Drawing (a half subject).

The importance of the subjects (1) and (2) is admitted by all. As regards subject (3) there is difference of opinion, but I have tried above to meet the reasons for excluding it, as far at least as Sanskrit and Arabic are concerned. The two parts of (4) are optional subjects at present, but I have given above my reasons for making them compulsory. Subject (5) is now partly compulsory and partly optional. But there are good reasons for including a portion of the existing optional part in the compulsory course. And I would make Drawing a compulsory subject on account of its general usefulness and its lending valuable aid to the study of science.

I shall next consider the question what should be the proper extent of each of the above mentioned subjects for the Matriculation standard.

This question is not very easy to answer, because conflicting considerations arise and there is no definite principle to guide us in fixing the limits of the standard in the different subjects. On the one hand, considering the advance that human knowledge has made in the last fifty years or so, the limits fixed more than half a century ago when the Calcutta University was established, must be raised. On the other hand, considering that life is short, and that the high pressure life of the present day has grown shorter, we can not conveniently prolong the period of pupilage, though art, always long, has grown longer still. How then are we to adjust the limits under these conflicting considerations?

The time limit cannot conveniently be raised, and I have suggested above, that fifteen years should be the average age limit for completing Secondary Education. If then the limits of the subjects are to be raised, we must be content either with reducing their number, that is, in other words, by allowing specialization, as the Calcutta University has done, by making History, Geography, and portions of Mathematics and Classics, optional subjects, or with only a moderate raising of the limits of the subjects, as I would suggest. In the higher stages of the student's progress, specialization must be allowed, and may well be allowed without causing any inconvenience. But to allow it in the lower stages would be positively injurious to all further progress. Different branches of knowledge are so intertwined with one another that in following any one of them we have often to come across one or more of the others. Even divergent subjects nave their points of convergence. One subject often requires to be illustrated by several others, and in its turn throws useful light upon those others. So that up to a certain stage, knowledge should stand on a broad basis to make progress upwards easy. Then again early specialization, though it may enable the student to know a great many truths of one or two subjects, will make his mind narrow, will stand in the way of his taking broad views of things and adapting himself to his environments, and will fail to attain one of the chief objects of General Education, which is to qualify a man to meet the emergencies of life by adapting himself to his surroundings or by changing them.

Retaining then the full complement of subjects as I have mentioned above, I would suggest that the extent of each for the Matriculation standard should be as indicated below.

In English, the first point to be settled is whether text-books should be prescribed or not. On this point, there is considerable difference of opinion. One view is that no text-books should be prescribed; a second view is that text-books should be prescribed; and a third view which is a compromise between the first and the second, with a strong leaning in favour of the first, is that a number of text-books may be recommended, but examiners may or may not, at their option, set passages for explanation from such books. The first view may be taken as the dominant view at the present day. It has the powerful support of the opinion of the majority of the Indian Universities Commission, with a dissentient minority of only one member. And the third view, which is the one adopted by the Calcutta University, is a compromise in appearance only between the other two views, but is in reality a carrying out of the first view.

With all respect for that view, I feel bound to say that it is not sound. I have stated at some length in my Note of Dissent from the Report of the Majority of the Indian Universities Commission my reasons for saying so, but as that Note may not be available to many, I shall here give the substance of my reasons for controverting that view.

The view is based upon three assumptions, namely, (1) that a student preparing for the Matriculation Examination should read English not so much to understand and appreciate English literature as to be able to express himself in English, to understand his text-books in other subjects written in English, and to follow the lectures of his professors at college;

(2) that if text-books in English are prescribed, that object will not be attained, as the student will cram the books instead of learning the language; and (3) that that object will be better secured by recommending for study a fairly large number of books so that it may not be possible for him to commit them all to memory. But these assumptions are all incorrect. In the first place, there is no reason why a Matriculation candidate should not begin to understand and appreciate literature. He has feelings though not all of them fully developed yet, and they should be cultured by suitable literature. In the second place, it is not correct to assume that the student will always try to memorize his text-book instead of understanding it and learning the language in which it is written. He does so, because wrong methods of teaching and examination are followed. If right methods are resorted to, he will try to understand and learn the language of his text-book and appreciate the literature it contains. And then there is no reason why memorizing, if it is intelligently done, should be held in such contempt. How except with the help of memory is a language to be learnt? Words must be remembered, phrases must be remembered, and even portions of sentences which involve peculiar idioms of a language should have to be remembered, if a language is to be learnt. And in the third place, it is clearly an error to assume that by recommending a long list of books in English for study, we help the Indian student to learn English, and prevent cramming. On the other hand, such a course will neither help the student in learning English properly nor will it prevent cramming. English is a difficult language for an Indian student to learn, owing to its vocabulary and its idioms being so different from those of the learner's vernacular. If then a large number of books is recommended for study, and if (as is inevitable) the student tries to read as many of them

as he possibly can, he will read them perfunctorily and with all the help that cramming can lend. On the other hand, if a small number of suitable books is prescribed, and if proper methods of teaching and examination are adopted, he will read those books carefully and intelligently, will appreciate their literary beauty, and will also learn better the language in which they are written, by having his attention detained longer over peculiarities of construction and idiom, than he can if he has a wider range of reading to go through, and a consequently smaller chance of having his attention arrested by peculiarities,

A great deal will depend upon the pieces selected. They should include both prose and poetry, but not drama nor works of literary criticism.

The pieces moreover should be so selected that they may serve other purposes as well, such as the teaching of important historical, or biographical, or geographical facts, or moral lessons. Again they should be such as are of cosmopolitan interest, that is interesting not merely to English boys, but to Indian boys as well. English literature is so vast and varied that with a little care, it will not be very difficult for well read scholars to make selections satisfying all these conditions.

In Classics, the present extent of the compulsory portion should be retained. More than that is not necessary, and less than that will not be sufficient.

In regard to the Vernaculars, I would suggest only one change, namely, that the maximum number of books that may be recommended, be reduced from six to three. My reason for suggesting the alteration is this, that the number six is somewhat large, and the recommendation of too many books imposes a heavy burden on the diligent, and scares away the lazy who (it is well known) do not read them at all, thinking that as they will be examined, not in the subject matter of the books but only as to their style, the knowledge they possess of their vernacular will be enough for them.

With regard to History, if Geography is to be included in this subject as I think it ought to be, the present syllabus should be reduced by the omission of some of the less important heads, such as detailed account of the Pathan period and of Mysore. And under Geography should be included only Descriptive Geography, but not Mathematical and Physical Geography.

Mathematics should, as at present, include Arithmetic, Algebra, and Geometry.

The course in Arithmetic should include the present compulsory portion, and the Extraction of Square Root in addition to it.

The course in Algebra should include the present compulsory portion and Quadratic Equations in addition to it.

The course in Geometry should include the present compulsory portion leaving out the part of the syllabus headed "Practical," and should include the portion of the syllabus for the optional paper headed "Theoretical" in addition to it.

Drawing should be a subject of study but not of Examination, except for those who wish to be examined in it.

On a consideration of the extent of the subjects as suggested above, it will be seen that the modified course will not be heavier than the present course, while it will have the advantage of being uniform and of being practically sufficient to qualify the student for his after career whatever that may be. The number of subjects remains five as before. The addition of Geography to History will be compensated by the reductions suggested in the History syllabus. The only real addition is in Mathematics, by the inclusion of Quadratic Equations and of the properties of Similar Triangles; but even that will to a large extent be compensated by the omission of Practical Geometry and Approximate Calculation.

Only a few words remain to be said about the nature of the tex-books for the Secondary Course. They should be written concisely but clearly, in simple but unambiguous language, and should be well illustrated by diagrams, maps, and pictures.

The text-books in English should not deal with any matter which will not be intelligible and interesting to Indian boys.

For the Matriculation course, the standard in prose may be roughly indicated by books like DeFoe's Robinson Crusoe, Lamb's Tales from Shakespeare, and Johnson's Rasselas; and the standard in poetry, by pieces like Gray's Elegy Written in a Country Churchyard, Goldsmith's Traveller and Deserted Village, and Longfellow's Psalm of Life. But books like Kipling's Jungle Book which are uninteresting, and like Macaulay's Lays of Ancient Rome which are full of obscure classical allusions, should not be recommended.

In History and Geography, books which enter too much into details should not be prescribed as text-books.

In Mathematics, no text-books need be prescribed for the Matriculation course, the syllabus given being sufficient to define the extent of the subject.

The foregoing are a few commonplace remarks on text books viewed purely from an intellectual point of view. The following are a few more remarks perhaps a little less commonplace, which I may here add with reference to text books viewed from political, moral, and religious points of view.

No book, whatever its other merits may be, should be prescribed as a text book, which tends directly or indirectly to encourage want of respect for constituted authority. This remark does not fully apply to any work on Political Philosophy which calmly and in a philosophic spirit deals with different forms of Government, discussing the merits and defects of each. The object of such a work is altogether different, and it is intended moreover for advanced students who can think and judge for themselves, and not for boys of immature minds who are liable to be easily misled. But while on the one hand we must take the utmost care to prevent books having any politically mischievous tendency from falling into the hands of young students, we should on the other hand avoid the opposite extreme of being needlessly nervous and taking exception to books like a poem on the Battle of Plassey, if the poet sheds a few pathetic tears over the tragic end of Siraj-ud-Dowla. Such tears will not move many hearts, and they will not do any harm.

From a moral point of view, we should exclude from the category of text books not only books that have an immoral tendency in the ordinary sense, but also those that teach by their example, habits of loose thinking, reckless writing, and pompous speaking. Books which spin out small matters to inordinate length, or complicate simple matters by affected pedantry of style, should be excluded. Books of this class fully verify the truth of the couplet,

> "Pride often guides the author's pen ;
> Books as often are affected as men."

For the same reason, books which indulge in vehement and unjust attack on an individual or a race should not be prescribed as text books. And Macaulay's Essay on Warren Hastings containing his well-known libel on Bengali character, notwithstanding the vigour and brilliancy of his style, should not find place in any list of text books at least for Bengali youth. Such books teach very little beyond the art of vituperation which no one stands much in need of learning.

Not much different from Macaulay's Essay on Warren Hastings is another notable work and a great work, Mill's History of British India,—great for its many merits, great for the greatness of its author, and great likewise for the boldness of its unmeasured vilification of the great and good things of ancient India of which its author knew so little. Speaking of Arjuna's Vision of the Image of God as displayed by the Universe, one of the sublimest things in Sanskrit literature, James Mill says, nothing could be more deformed and monstrous, because his finite mind could not find anything methodical and orderly in that image of the Infinite. As well might one complain, as some have complained, that there is no order or design in creation, because in the very limited portion of the universe within our limited ken, the stars appear to be scattered at random and not arranged in regular geometrical figures. James Mill's History is not a little responsible for that prejudice and want of sympathy which many young English Civilians show towards Indians. This is what Mr. Horace Hayman Wilson, Mill's countrymen and Editor of his History, says of the book :—" Considered merely in a literary capacity, the description of the Hindus in the History of British India is open to censure for its obvious unfairness and injustice; but in the effect it is likely to exercise upon the connexion between the people of England and the people of India, it is chargeable with more than literary demerit; the tendency is evil; it is calculated to destroy all sympathy between the rulers and the ruled; to preoccupy the minds of those who issue annually from Great Britain to monopolize the posts of honour and power in Hindustan with an unfounded aversion towards those over whom they exercise that power and from whom they enforce that honour; and to substitute for those generous and benevolent feelings which the situation of the younger servants of the Company in India naturally suggests, sentiments of disdain, suspicion and dislike, uncongenial to their age and character, and wholly incompatible with the full and faithful discharge of their obligations to Government and to the people."

Text books may be open to objection also on religious

grounds. An Elementary History of England was objected to by certain Jesuit Fathers on the ground of its being unfair towards Roman Catholics, and the objection had to be given effect to. On another occasion, a text book of Geography was objected to, because speaking of the Ganges it said that there was no teason for regarding that river as an object of veneration ; and the objection prevailed irrespective of the question whether that statement in the book was right or wrong, and solely on the ground that, it was injurious to the growth of the feeling of reverence in the student, if he was to be told by his parents at 8 o'clock in the morning to hold the Ganges in veneration, and to be taught by his teacher two or three hours later that quite the contrary was true. One of Bacon's Essays was taken exception to for speaking irreverently of the Prophet of Islam, and the objection prevailed. A work on Comparative Religion may dispassionately discuss the merits and defects of different religions ; but a literary work has not the same privilege. A work on anatomy may contain a sketch of nude human body, but in an illustrated literary work such a sketch would be intolerable.

The Higher or Collegiate stage. I come now to the Higher or Collegiate stage of General Education. And the first question here is, whether there should be a bifurcation between Arts and Science, and if so, should it begin from the very beginning of the Collegiate Course?

Though the distinction between Arts and Science as usually drawn is not a strictly logical distinction, and though there is considerable overlapping of parts in the Arts and Science Courses of our Universities, yet the distinction has obtained so long and is become so popular, that there is little chance of the bifurcation between Arts and Science being given up or even put off till a higher stage of progress than that at which it begins. Nor does it matter much practically whether the distinction should be retained and from what stage, so long as the courses of study in Arts and Science consist of proper groups of subjects. As my object is only to secure some practical good, I must proceed along lines of least resistance, and I would accept the bifurcation of the courses of study into Arts and Science from the commencement of the Collegiate stage.

Proceeding upon that basis, the questions that we have to consider are,

(1) What should the duration of the Collegiate Course up to the time of graduation be?

(2) What should the subjects be and how far should there be alternative optional subjects?

(3) What should the extent of each subject be?

The question, what should be the nature of the text books, need not be considered here again, as I have already said all that I wish to say about text-books when dealing with Secondary Education.

(1) *Duration of the Collegiate Course.*—The duration of the Collegiate Course is usually extended over four years from Matriculation to first graduation, and is divided into two periods of two years each; and a further period of two years is added to it for those who go up for the Master's degree in Arts or Science. In the case of private, that is non-collegiate, students, this last mentioned period is required by the Calcutta University to be three years.

The only alteration I have to suggest regarding these periods of study, is, that there should be no distinction between collegiate and private students preparing for the higher degree examination, and that the period should be two years in all cases.

(2) *Subjects of Examination.*

Subjects for the I. A. and I. Sc. Examinations.—The next question is, what should the subjects for the Intermediate Examinations in Arts and Science be. In the Calcutta University, the number of subjects is five for each of these two Examinations. But the different options allowed go to make the scheme embarrassingly complicated, it being possible for a candidate for the Intermediate Arts Examination to choose any one out of as many as forty-six different combinations of subjects, and for an Intermediate Science Examination candidate to select any one out of thirty-six different combinations. The object of giving such wide range of choice is, to make the course suit different tastes and capacities. But the result of allowing such a wide range of choice is, in the first place, to bewilder and puzzle students and their advisers; in the second place, to embarrass colleges in the preparation of their time tables, and to impair the efficiency of their teachers; and in the third place, to lead students to select strange combinations of subjects, they being influenced in the choice of their subjects, not so much by their aptitude for the study of the subjects as by the consideration whether the question papers of previous years in any subject were easy or difficult. The allowing of options, therefore, practically leads to little good and to much evil. It will be certainly better to prescribe only a small number of reasonable combinations of subjects.

I would suggest that the number of subjects should be five for both the examinations, and that the subjects for the two examinations be grouped as follows:—

For the Intermediate Examination in Arts—

1. English Language and Literature (One full subject).
2. A Vernacular (A half subject).
3. Logic (A half subject).
4. Mathematics (One full subject).

5. One of the following subjects :—
   (*i*) A Classical Language.
   (*ii*) History.
   (*iii*) Physics.
   (*iv*) Chemistry.

For the Intermediate Examination in Science.—

1. English Language and Literature (One full subject).
2. A Vernacular (A half subject).
3. Logic (A half subject).
4. Mathematics (One full subject).
5. One of the following subjects :—
   (*i*) Physics.
   (*ii*) Chemistry.
   (*iii*) Biology (Botany and Physiology.)
   (*iv*) Geology.

A sixth subject namely, Physiology, should be a subject of Study but not of Examination in each of the two courses.

I have already given in general terms my reasons for restricting the choice of subjects within reasonable limits; and I shall now shortly state my reasons for adopting the particular combinations mentioned above.

English is a necessary subject of study for every Indian student, for two obvious reasons. In the first place, it is the medium of communication between him and his rulers and members of the ruling race, and so a good knowledge of it is good preparation for the discharge of his duties as a citizen. And in the second place, it is the medium through which he must, at least for some time (that is until his vernaculars attain greater development) receive instruction in the higher branches of knowledge.

The student's Vernacular must also be a subject of study, to enable him to hold his place in the polished society of his countrymen, and to disseminate among his less educated countrymen the knowledge he acquires by his better education.

Logic as the science of the laws of thought and as dealing with the rules of correct reasoning, deductive and inductive, ought to be read by every student. It is true that one may think and reason correctly without knowing Logic; but a knowledge of Logic is a great help to every one who has to think and reason, to enable him to avoid falling into error himself, and to detect errors in others, in thinking and reasoning. Logic moreover is an interesting subject, and elementary Logic is not very difficult.

So far there will not be much difference of opinion. But in regard to Mathematics, there is great divergence of views. While some consider it a very useful subject, others think that it is necessary only for students of Physics, and that it is unnessary for others, and is a stumbling block to many. Let us pause for a minute to examine the matter closely.

In the first place, we should draw a distinction between Elementary Mathematics such as can form part of the course for the Intermediate Examination, and Higher Mathematics which may be prescribed for the B. A. Honour and the M. A. Examination, and it may be readily conceded that all minds have not equal capacity or aptitude for the study of the latter; but it cannot as readily be admitted that every ordinary sound mind has not the capacity for the study of the former. Experience proves that with a little patience and perseverance, every ordinary sound mind can learn Elementary Mathemetics, and that the aversion shown to Mathematics is often the result, either of prejudice created by wrong notions instilled into the mind, or of disinclination for that sustained attention which Mathematics requires, or of bad teaching at an early stage which may create a lasting distaste for the subject. I may here refer to an instance which occurred in my own experience, and which is only one of many instances that must have come to the notice of almost every teacher of Mathematics. When I was Lecturer on Mathematics in the Presidency College in 1865, the late Mr. Romesh Chunder Dutt, afterwards a member of the Civil Service, was a student of the first year class. I used to set a few exercises to be worked out by the students at home. Finding on two successive days that Mr. Dutt did not work out any of the exercises set, I asked him the reason for his neglect of work, and was told that he had no aptitude for Mathematics. I then told him somewhat sternly that it did not require the genius of a Newton or a Laplace to understand the Elementary Mathematics taught in the first year college class, and that every man of sound mind could understand it if only he would try to do so. Mr. Dutt felt the rebuke, for his eyes became moist. I relented, and gently advised him to try to work out only the first two or three exercises set for the next day that were easy. The next day with a smiling face he showed me his exercise book and said he had worked out the easy exercises and also some of the more difficult ones, and from that day his progress in Mathematics was found to be certainly not below the average.

Speaking of students who find it difficult to understand Mathematics, Poincare in his "Science and Method" (p. 118) remarks, "Almost all are more exacting; they want to know not only whether all the syllogisms of a demonstration are correct, but why they are linked together in one order rather than in another. * * * * *

* * * * * *

As they advance further, they will no longer see even this ephemeral light, because the theorems depend upon one another, and those they require have been forgotten. Thus it is that they become incapable of understanding mathematics." And a little further on, he adds, "Others will always ask themselves what use it is. They will not have understood, unless they find around them, in practice or in nature, the object of such and such mathematical notion." And I may add that there are others again who think or are encouraged to think, that the study of Mathematics is dull drudgery unworthy of their fiery intellect which should soar unrestrained to sublime heights of fancy; while there are not a few who give up the study of Mathematics in despair, on being told by those who ought to have encouraged them, that the subject is too subtle for their obtuse intellect.

Thus the difficulty in the study of Elementary Mathematics will on examination be found to be more apparent than real, the only real difficulty being the inability of some minds to maintain close and sustained attention to anything for any length of time. The power of close attention is necessary not only for success in mathematical study, but for success in every other work of life, and mathematical study is the best training for the acquisition of the habit of close and continued attention.

Some educationists think, that this view is erroneous and is a survival of the old Faculty Psychology, that there is no faculty of attention which can be trained generally, and that each man attends only to that which has interest for him. That may be quite true. But interest in different things, and interest in noting nice distinctions and minute details, and in following long chains of reasoning generally, may be created by training. And the study of Mathematics has been found most effective in giving such training.

The fact is undeniable, and its explanation apart from any faculty psychology theory would be this: A student of Mathematics finds by repeated trials the necessity of noting nice distinctions and minute details, and of attending to long chains of close reasoning, and the danger of falling into egregious errors by neglecting to note such distinctions and details and to follow such reasoning, and when he comes to deal with any other subject of study or any matter of business, the memory of his experience in mathematical study makes him realize the necessity of following the same course in his new work, and the realization of this necessity creates the desired interest.

That habits of close reasoning and power of critical analysis acquired by training in one subject, can be useful in dealing with another and a quite diffierent subject, may be illustrated by an example like the following. In a trial for attempt to murder by poisoning with arsenic, one of the witnesses for the prosecution was a chemist who had analysed part of tbe alleged poisoned drink, and who said that he had discovered traces of arsenic in it, and to negative the possibility of its being supposed that the test tubes used might have contained traces of the poison, he added they had been carefully washed. The counsel for the accused in his cross-examination asked the chemist whether he had tested the water with which he washed the test tubes, and could be sure that it did not contain any trace of arsenic, and his answer was in the negative, and thus a small loop-hole was left in the evidence. The lawyer who was accustomed to sift and analyse evidence in court, had acquired a power which could be of use to the chemist in his laboratory.

Besides this indirect value of the study of Mathematics for the training it gives to the mind, it has also a direct value for the truths it teaches, which are of useful application, not only in the study of Physics, but also in many of the ordinary affairs of life. The Mathematics learned in the Secondary stage of Education may, it is true, be sufficient for most purposes : but there are purposes for which a little more knowledge of Mathematics is not only useful but necessary, in these days when the practical applications of science are multiplying fast to minister to our comforts, and even to supply our daily wants. Some knowledge of solid geometry, of logarithmic computation, and of trigonometrical ratios, will be found useful for many ordinary purposes.

I would therefore make Mathematics a compulsory subject for the Intermediate Examinations in Arts and Science.

In the Arts course for the Intermediate Examination, either a Classical Language or History will form an appropriate fifth subject. And as there are many students who, though they intend to take up the Arts course, are yet anxious to learn something about one Science subject at least, it is deemed desirable to give them the option of studying one of the two most important Science subjects, Physics and Chemistry, as the fifth subject.

In the Science course, an appropriate fifth subject will be one of the following four, namely,

Physics (the science of general properties of material bodies).

Chemistry (the science of the internal composition of material bodies).

Biology (the science of living bodies),

Geology (the science of the structure, composition and other properties of the Earth we inhabit).

Regarding the extent of the subjects, I think the limits fixed by our University may be accepted as proper, they being neither too high nor too low.

Besides the five Examination subjects, I have included in the Intermediate Course in Arts and in Science, a sixth subject Physiology, as a subject for Study but not for Examination. The subject is one of very great importance. Every student ought to know something of his own body. And the importance of the subject and the interest it will have for every student, will ensure its attentive study notwithstanding that no examination will have to be passed in it. The extent of the subject (Physiology) should be that preseribed by the Calcutta University.

Subjects for the B. A. and B. Sc. Examinations. The next question is what should be the subjects for the B. A. and B. Sc. Examinations.

The first point for determination is as to the number of subjects to be included in the course. The old idea of a scholar was epigrammatically expressed by the well known sentence, "A scholar should know something of every thing and every thing of something." With the rapid advance that human knowledge has made since that definition was first given, it is become almost impossible to have any scholar answering that description. When the Calcutta University was established, the number of subjects for the B. A. Examination was six, namely, (1) English, (2) A second language (Classical or Vernacular), (3) History, (4) Philosophy (that is Mental and Moral Philosophy and Logic), (5) Mathematics and (6) Natural and Physical Science (that is Chemistry, Chemical Physics, Zoology and Physical Geography), and for the M. A. Examination, the course consisted of any one of those six subjects. That arrangement worked fairly well more than half a century ago, but it will not do so at the present day. Six subjects will be too many to be studied even if the extent of each be moderate only, compared with the extent to which the domain of human knowledge has advanced. On the other hand, up to the B. A. or B. Sc. stage, it is not desirable to limit the number of subjects to one or even two. Our graduates are to be trained not as artisans to acquire a high degree of skill in one particular line of work, but as men of culture capable of discharging properly the multifarious duties of a citizen in modern civilized society. For that purpose they must have breadth of culture, and their courses of study should cover a fair extent of surface even at some sacrifice of depth, which should be left to be reached in the M. A. or M. Sc. stage. Three subjects with the student's vernacular as a half subject, will be a fair number to fix upon.

What then are to be the three subjects for the B. A. and the B. Sc. course respectively, and what should be the extent of option allowed in regard to the subjects? The Calcutta University, while limiting the number of subjects as I have suggested, allows options to a bewildering extent. In the B. A. course, the number of options allowed is thirty five, and in the B. Sc. course, it is as many as fiftysix. Nor are all the possible combinations of subjects helpful to students in their acquisition of systematic knowledge. The objections which I have urged against allowing too many options in the selection of subjects, when considering the Intermediate Examination courses, apply with still greater force to the B. A. and B. Sc. courses.

The following will, I think, be a much better scheme of subjects than the one now adopted for the B. A. and B. Sc. courses.

B. A. Course :

1. English.
2. Mental and Moral Science.
3. One of the following :
   (*a*) A Classical Language.
   (*b*) History and Economics.
   (*c*) Mathematics.
4. The student's Vernacular (A Half subject).

B. Sc. Course :

1. English.
2. Mathematics.
3. One of the following :
   (*a*) Physics and Chemistry.

(*b*) Physiology and Botany.

(*c*) Geology and Mineralogy.

4. The student's Vernacular (A Half subject).

That English and the student's Vernacular should form part of the B. A. Course will I think be admitted by every one. I would make Mental Science and Moral Science also compulsory subjects, partly for their direct value in teaching important truths, and partly for their indirect value as disciplinary study. One of the remaining three subjects will form the third full subject.

The question whether English and the student's Vernacular should form parts of the B. Sc. Course is one upon which there is much difference of opinion. Many educationists maintain that as the language of Science is technical and sometimes symbolical, knowledge of English and Vernacular is not necessary for the student of Science. I do not think that this view is correct. For the Indian student, English is a difficult foreign language for the thorough understanding of which, a little more knowledge of it than what is acquired in the Intermediate Examination stage, is not only desirable but necessary. Then there are many standard works on Science for the proper study of which a good knowledge of English will be a useful equipment. And if one of the objects of the Indian student of Science is to popularize Science among his countrymen, cultivation of his Vernacular also is necessary for the attainment of that object.

I would make Mathematics also a compulsory subject for the B. S. Course, partly on account of its indirect value as a disciplinary subject of study, but mainly on account of its direct value as teaching truths which are necessary to be known by the student of Science. It is not correct to say that Physics is the only branch of Science for the study of which a knowledge of Mathematics above the Intermediate Course is necessary. Some knowledge of Hydrostatics which is outside the Intermediate Course, is necessary for the proper study of even such an apparently non-mathematical subject as Physiology. But to suit non-mathematical students I would suggest a small reduction in in the course prescribed by our University, by substituting Descriptive Astronomy for Astronomy treated mathematically, and by omitting Summation of Series from Trigonometry. This alteration will slightly reduce the extent of the course without materially affecting its value.

In addition to the Pass Course for the B. A. and B. Sc. Examinations, students should, as heretofore, be permitted to take up the Honours Course in one of the subjects.

Upon the question of the extent of the subjects for the B. A and B. Sc. Courses, I have not much to say. I would accept the limits fixed by the Calcutta University, with the slight modification in Mathematics suggested above, and with a general qualification all round to the effect, that within the limits prescribed, each subject should be studied so as to ensure a rational understanding of broad principles as distinguished from a mere mechanical knowledge of minute details.

Before leaving the consideration of the under-graduate stage of Collegiate Education, I wish to make one more suggestion of general interest. I have already said at the outset of my remarks on Collegiate Education that the distinction between an Arts Course and a Science Course is not a clearly and logically well sustained one, but that there is considerable overlapping of the two, and that I accept the division between the two out of deference to prevailing sentiment. And I must here add that our recognition of that distinction should not lead us to throw unnecessary difficulties in the way of honest and diligent students. Now one such unnecessary difficulty is created by the Regulations of the Calcutta University, which require that if a candidate for the B. A. Examination has passed the Intermediate Examination not in Arts but in Sciene, he must pass an Examination in one of the Arts subjects for the Intermediate Examination, and that if a candidate for the B. Sc. Examination has passed the Intermediate Examination not in Science but in Arts, he must pass the Intermediate Examination in Science, receiving only the concession that he will be excused one year's study, and also attendance and examination in any Science subject in which he has already passsed at the Intermediate Examination in Arts.

The conditions imposed upon candidates going from the Science to the Arts side and *vice versa* are unnecessary. In the former case the condition serves no purpose, as the candidate may pass in one Arts subject for the Intermediate Examination and take up another Arts subject for the B. A. Examination; and so in the second case he may take up one Science subject for the Intermediate and another for the B. Sc. Examination. A candidate who has passed the Intermediate Examination either in Arts or in Science, has had full training for two years, and if he changes his Course from Arts to Science or *vice versa* at the B.Sc. or B. A. Examination stage, he will again have full preparatory training for two years, and he may be fairly presumed to be able to profit by such training; and we may credit a student at his age with sense enough to understand his own interest, and may spare ourselves the trouble of encumbering him with unnecessary directions to help him. Nor must we think that he changes his course out of mere caprice. There are often good reasons for his doing so. He may find from experience in the Intermediate stage that he has better aptitude for Arts subjects than for Science subjects which he took up, or the reverse, and he may therefore think it desirable to change his course at the final stage, when he has still a period of two years for preparatory training; or he may find it impossible to obtain admission in any college which teaches the group of subjects he intends to take up for the B.A. or the B. Sc. Course, and to avoid the necessity of taking up another group of subjects which does not suit him well, he may feel forced to change his course to find a group that suits him better.

With regard to the Post-graduate Courses, that is the M. A and M. Sc. Courses, I have not much to say. These courses are very properly limited to single subjects, or where the subjects are large, to single branches of subjects, with a view to secure depth of culture. And the Regulations of our University justly permit candidates in certain subjects to substitute Research work for a part of the Examination. I have only two remarks to make with reference to the M. A. Course and Research work.

In the first place, I do not think it desirable to prescribe for the M. A. Examination any course the study of which will not be profitable in the fullest sense of the word. Deep learning and deep thinking in any branch of knowledge is good but remembering that life is short, while art is long, and remembering also that in the short span of human life, man has many things to do, it will not be wise to devote our time and energy to the study of any branch of knowledge without discrimination. From this point of view, I think groups D, E, and F of the M. A. Course in Sanskrit may be omitted, and group C modified by substituting in head (b) of Papers VI and VII something more of standard works in Nyaya and Vedanta in the place translation from English into Sanskrit. This alteration in the Sanskrit Philosophy Course which will give the student a general view of different systems, will make the study of Hindu Philosophy more useful than a deep but exclusive study of any single system.

And in the second place, while research work should be encouraged in every possible way, we should be careful to secure real research work, and not to allow it to degenerate into a mere name.

Some educationists think that the discovery of any new truth, however valueless or insignificant it may now appear, deserves the name of Research. According to them, the discovery of any new property of a known curve, or of a new form of star on the wing of a butterfly, would be Research work. For they say, when Apollonius of Perga discovered the properties of the Conic Sections, no one anticipated that they would help Kepler in formulating his laws, which again helped Newton in explaining the mechanics of the Solar System. That is quite true. But times are changed. We now live under high pressure, we want things of immediate use, and we can not remain long in expectancy, treasuring up truths and waiting for some happy day when they may turn out to be of use.

What I have just said about Research work applies also to the thesis required from candidates for the Doctor's Degree, which is to be based upon the discovery of new facts observed by the candidate himself or of new relations of facts observed by others. The new facts or new relations of facts should be important and useful, aud the mere fact of their being new should not be enough. If human life was as long now as it was in the days of the patriarchs, and if pressure of work had not increased as it has now, every fact of Nature and every fact of History would have been interesting study. But in the circumstances in which we are how placed, it is only such facts of Nature and of History as can help to elucidate the present or improve the future of man, that are worth enquiring into, and much that is being written is mere waste of time and energy. And my only answer to the curt retort which may turn this remark against thé writing embodying the remark, would be that, that writing is not long, and does not therefore involve much waste of time and energy,

(2) *Professional Education,*

The consideration of Professional Education will not detain me long Of the three branches of it, namely, Law, Medicine, and Engineering, it is only the first regarding which I can speak usefully as to details; the other two I can discuss only with reference to their general principles. All that I propose to do would be, to consider a few general principles relating to the three branches, and then to make one or two suggestions in matters of details regarding the first.

As all these professions are becoming over-crowded, one important question for consideration is, how to stop further over-crowding. It is suggested by some that entrance into them should be made difficult by artificial checks, such as by making Professional Education more expensive. I think that would be unjust and undesirable. Over-crowding is no doubt an evil in itself, as it lowers the dignity of a profession by reducing its emoluments and thereby making it less attractive to deserving persons. It leads also to evil consequences by driving the members of a profession to improper conduct. Overcrowding of professions should, therefore, in the interests of the public and of the professions themselves, be prevented as far as possible by all legitimate means. But the proposed remedy of making Professional Education unnecessarily expensive, is not in any sense a legitimate means, and should not therefore be resorted to. Many of the brightest ornaments of the learned professions have been furnished by the poorer classes of society, and their pursuit of knowledge under difficulties furnishes some of the noblest examples of the triumph of man over adverse environments. The true remedy against over-crowding of the learned professions lies in gradually raising the requisite standard of proficiency, so that none but the really deserving may enter, while none among the really deserving will be shut out.

Another general question of principle relating to Professional Education is, as to the extent to which State interference should be considered proper.

Considering the grave nature of the responsibility undertaken by medical and legal practitioners who are entrusted with life and property, it is desirable in the highest degree that the public should have some guarantee of their character and qualification before they are licensed to practise. An engineer also undertakes responsibility, though perhaps not as grave, and if a house or a bridge which he may unskilfully build, collapses, loss of live and property may be the result. So some guarantee of fitness is necessary in his case also.

As regards legal practitioners, there is no difficulty or difference of opinion in this matter. They derive their authority to practise from Courts of Justice, which test their fitness by their University degrees and by other tests specially prescribed. The only point on which some difference of opinion exists, is whether Law graduates only should be allowed to practise, or whether others also should be licensed to practise in the lower Courts, after satisfying a less severe test than an examination for a Law degree. The number of Law graduates is becoming so large that it is neither necessary nor desirable that an inferior class of men should be licensed to practise as pleaders.

The licensing of medical practitioners involves great difficulty, and has given rise to much difference of opinion. The first question is, whether medical practitioners should be required to go through any course of training and to satisfy any test, before they are licensed to practise. Grave as their responsibility is, Indian society has practically answered that question in the negative. And the reason for it is evident. There are now prevailing four well known systems of Medicine, namely, the Allopathic, the Homœopathic, the Ayurvedic, and the Unany, besides certain others less known. Of these, neither Government nor the Universities recognize any but the first. There are a few institutions more or less well organized for teaching the second and the third system. But there is none that I know of for teaching the fourth. And it should be remembered that the third and also the fourth are systems which have long been prevailing. Moreover the first two systems do not furnish practitioners enough to satisfy the requirements of the people. In this state of things, any one who professes to practise any system of Medicine, and who has fair intelligence and some knowledge of his system, has a good chance of success. This state of things will I fear continue. Compulsory measures will not remedy the evil, but will on the contrary lead to hardship not only on honest practitioners but also on the public. The only remedy against the spread of quackery that can be suggested, will be the establishment by voluntary effort of well conducted institutions in all great cities for imparting instruction in Medicine according to the different systems, the formation of voluntary associations of men learned in the different systems to exercise control over those institutions, and the granting of diplomas to qualified students after testing their fitness.

Another and much narrower question is, whether in the orthodox or Allopathic system, the right to practise should be confined to graduates in Medicine, or whether a lower grade of medical practitioners should also be recognized, and if recognized, by what authority should they be licensed to practise. Having regard to the comparatively small number of our graduates in Medicine, and to the large number and indigent condition of those who require medical aid, it is clear that we require a lower grade of medical men in addition to graduates. This is admitted by all. But there is difference of opinion as regards the authority from which the lower grade of medical men should receive their license to practise. Some hold that the function of the University is limited to granting degrees, but that it is no part of the business of a University to grant people license to practise, and that it is the province of Government to establish a Medical Council for granting such license; while others maintain that it is the University as the highest educational agency that snould determine the educational fitness not only of graduates in Medicine but also of those seeking to obtain license to practise. As the question of granting license to practise Medicine is one in which the public is more interested than the Government, I think the power to grant license should belong not to the Government but to the University in which Government control is leavened to some extent by the popular element.

With regard to Education in Engineering, all I wish to say is that it should be imparted by institutions affiliated to and controlled by the Universities. Government control is good, but University control which combines Government control with some measure of popular control, is better, in respect of matters in which the Government and the public are both interested.

Coming now to questions of detail, the only suggestion I have to make, relates to the provision for attendance at Moot Courts as part of Legal Education. I would suggest that that provision be altogether left out. It entails expenditure of time and energy without giving any adequate return in the shape of improvement in ability or increase of attainments. Indeed in one sense it is worse than useless; for it is likely to lower the student's sense of the seriousness of Law study. Little boys and girls may imitate business of life in play because they are unfit for actual business; sham fight may be resorted to in training soldiers for actual fight, because actual battle is a dangerous experiment. But Law students need not be taken through sham Courts when real Courts are open to them to resort to, and to see how proceedings are actually conducted there. If it is said that students cannot actually take part in the business of real Courts, the answer is, no more can all of them do so in the Moot Courts, where only some few actually talk and act, while the majority merely listen and see.

(3) *Technical Education.*—In these days of keen competition and severe struggle for existence, the importance of Technical Education can hardly be overrated. It is Technical Education which alone can furnish a solution of the bread problem, and can relieve General Education and Professional Education from their state of congestion.

While the supply of men for the civil service (in its widest sense), the only field open to recipients of General Education, is far in excess of the demand, and while the learned professions are all more or less overcrowed, people in this country are still anxious to receive General or Professional Education, and there is very little advance towards Technical Education; and yet almost every one knows that it is only Technical Education that qualifies men to produce and distribute the necessaries of life. The question therefore presses itself upon our attention,—Why is this, and how are we to popularize Technical Education? One ready answer is,—Necessity will drive men to seek for Technical Education, and it is not necessary to inquire why they have not hitherto sought for it. It is quite true that in the self-adjusting economy of Nature, no evil can be permanent, and those suffering from any evil must either mend or end. But that is not a very cheering prospect either way. To end, no one would wish, and to mend, driven by sheer necessity, would involve serious sacrifice. It is therefore better to inquire into the first part of the question, with a view to answer the second, before matters proceed further from bad to worse.

The people of India, as indulgent children of a bounteous Nature, have been a peace loving unadventurous and contemplative race. The absence of want, the presence of leisure, and the influence of temperament produced by the food they took, inclined them to spiritual culture, which has produced a system of philosophy remarkable for its effect in restraining selfish instincts and love of transitory pleasures. But their veneration for the past kept each caste to its customary calling, and that helped to improve arts and industries, and to advance gradually though slowly the material prosperity of the country. When however with the accession of British Rule, a new and unquestionably bright era dawned on the country, and some of its old institutions and old ideas were swept away by Western Education and Western notions, caste distinctions lost their rigidity, and all classes claimed equality of treatment; and then it was that the sense of dignity attaching to occupations of the higher castes appealed to men's minds, and thus arose that scramble by all castes for employment in the civil service and in the learned professions to the neglect of agriculture and manufacture, the evil consequences of which are now so evident. Though hereditary caste distinction is practically gone, professional caste distinction still continues, and the dignity of labour has not yet been fully recognized. That is why, though starvation is staring us in the face, we are still desparately scrambling for place in fields where there is absolutely no vacant space, and avoiding fields which promise a fair harvest.

False sentiment is thus one main cause of the unpopularity of Technical Education. It should be discouraged and it will die out in the end. But in the meantime, we may, I think, adopt measures which will not only remove all sentimental objection against receiving Technical Education, but will place the imparting of it on an efficient footing.

I would suggest that a Faculty of Technology, including Agriculture and Mining, Manufacture and Commerce, or at least a Faculty of Agriculture, be constituted in each of our Universities, and Colleges be established and affiliated to the Universities for imparting instruction in those subjects, so that students belonging to the *Bhadralok* or genteel classes may take to technological pursuits and yet attain the rank of undergraguates and graduates. I know that this suggestion will be at once met by the objection that it is no part of the business of a University to constitute new Faculties to foster false sentiment, and that if people want Technical Education, they should found Schools and Colleges for imparting such Education, and should not wait for the Universities to take the initiative. And the suggestion may provoke the ever ready ridicule of one section of our critics who say, that our students are a race of degree hunters who want not knowledge but a cheap degree, and for whom an appropriate University will be one that grants a degree on payment of a small fee without insisting on any thing more. I will not quarrel with those critics. Our young men who have not many fields open to them to give their aspirations full play, have, it may be admitted, the ambition, honest and excusable though it be, to obtain University degrees. But all ambition is weakness, and every manifestation of weakness must excite laughter and ridicule in those who are free from it. This is according to psychologists the philosophical explanation of laughter, and laws of psychology are inexorable laws of Nature with which it is vain to contend.

While leaving our humorous critics to enjoy their mirth at the expense of my young countrymen, I would beg of our more serious critics to bear in mind that even adventurous English youths with so many fields open to them for the gratification of their ambition, keenly aspire after becoming University men, and that Faculties of Agriculture and Commerce are not altogether unheard of things, but form part of many modern Universities. India or at any rate Bengal is an eminently agricultural country, and agricultural Education will be a valuable training for Bengali youths, and will enable them to find profitable employment for themselves, and to add to the real wealth of the country. There is one great advantage which Agriculture has in this country over other technological pursuits. There is plenty of culturable land available to begin with. And then Agriculture does not require investment of much capital, or the employment of much skilled labour. So that young men of the poorer middle classes can take to Agriculture easily, if only they are fitted by proper training. I would therefore once more earnestly repeat my suggestion for the constitution of a Faculty of Agriculture by our Universities, and for the establishment of institutions for imparting instruction in Agriculture.

In the departments of Manufacture and Commerce, Indian students specially in Bengal, labour under many disadvantages which must not be lost sight of by organizers of Technical Education. Practical training in Manufacture and Commerce can be given only by making students work as apprentices in manufactories and mercantile firms. But the great majority of these are owned by Europeans, and they naturally feel great disinclination to admit Indian apprentices. Nor can model manufactories and model mercantile firms for the training of students be opened as easily as model farms. So that it is not easy to give our students necessary training in these subjects.

Nor again is it easy for those few who have managed to acquire the necessary training, to find suitable employment, as the employers of skilled labour in these departments, who are mostly Europeans, do not like to employ Indians except in the lower grades. And we cannot expect Indian students who generally come from the poorer classes, to find funds wherewith to start manufacturing or commercial business on their own account. In this state of things, until Indians directly invest their capital more largely in manufacture, the only sort of Education in Manufacture that will be profitable, is training in cottage industries with machine tools, so that trained students may with small capital start business on their own account and earn their living. I would accordingly suggest that Education in Manufacture should for the present proceed mainly upon the lines indicated above.

In the department of Commerce, Education need not be cut down in any way; but until Indian capital flows largely into that channel, our students shall have to remain content with getting employment only as clerks.

III. Moral Education.—The problem of organizing a system of Moral Education is a difficult one in every country, and is specially so in India. The inherent difficulty of the problem arises from the fact that the importance of Moral Education is not generally recognized, but on the contrary, Moral Education is considered unnecessary and useless, unnecessary for the majority of mankind who are believed to be good enough without such education, and useless for the small minority who are taken to be so bad as to be past reformation. And efforts to give Moral Education are sometimes resented by popular sentiment as implying an unmerited slur on humanity, and evoke sarcasms like the remark that you cannot make men moral by Act of Parliament. And as morality is closely connected with religion, and derives its best if not its sole ultimate support from religion, the fact of the great diversity of religions prevailing in India, constitutes the special difficulty of the Moral Education problem in this country.

But these difficulties must be met, the importance of Moral Education must be recognized, and steps must be taken in the best interests of society for imparting such education. The truth is that man is neither so good as to make Moral Education unnecessary, nor so bad as to make it useless. The few fundamental truths of morality which may be intuitively known by the human mind, might have been sufficient for unsophisticated man in simple primitive society. But man with his mind sophisticated by false culture, and his physical wants needlessly multiplied by an enervating civilization, has his selfish instincts so strongly stimulated, that moral training is become absolutely necessary to guide him through the complicated maze of modern social relations. I shall give two instances to make my meaning clear. As they are recent, to avoid giving offence to any one I will omit names.

One of these is an instance in which a public meeting was announced to be held in a hall not very large at which a very distinguished popular leader and orator was to address the student community. Long before the appointed hour, the hall was filled, and the footpath in front crowded. The convener of the meeting then forbade further entry into the hall, and when inspite of that, some students entered, he roughly handled (so the report goes), or used offensive language to, one of them. Thereupon all the students left the hall, and kept waiting on the footpath till the arrival of the lecturer, and then they asked him to deliver his address in an open public place that was close by. The convener of the meeting apologized to the students for what he had done, and the lecturer requested them to enter the hall once more in deference to the wish of the convener, and then walk out to the open space where he would deliver his address. But they declined to do this, and so the meeting was not held. This gave rise to public criticism of the conduct of both sides.

The object of all concerned was good in the beginning; a little want of foresight in the convener of the meeting brought about a difficulty; and in doing what the parties did in that situation, every one thought he was doing what was right. But (I speak subject to correction) there were mistakes on both sides. On the side of the convener of the meeting, it is said that when he found the crowd larger than his hall could accommodate, he was bound in the interests of order and discipline to prevent further entry, while on the part of the students, it is urged that having invited them to come, he had no right to prevent their entry, and that after he had insulted them, sense of self-respect required them to refuse to enter his hall again. Here is a case in which the moral questions arising are of some nicety. Each party may be credited with having acted according to the best of his lights. But a little more light might have helped the parties to avoid the unpleasant affair altogether, or to make it end pleasantly. The little light that is in me leads me to say (subject to correction of course), that the better course for the convener of the meeting was, not strong remonstrance with his invited guests asking any of them to leave the hall, but gentle persuasion asking them to help him out of the difficulty which he did not anticipate; and the better course for the students was not to seek to force their entry into the hall after the prohibition (whether right or wrong) of the person in charge of it, and not to show want of respect to the lecturer who had given no offence, and want of forgiveness to the convener after he had apologized. Assertion of right is good, but self-abnegation is better. Sense of self-respect is good, but spirit of forgiveness is better. And Moral Education may help one to realize that.

The other instance I wish to give is one in which a convict, who was an educated man, murdered a fellow prisoner to prevent his giving evidence as an approver in a case of anarchist conspiracy; and some well behaved young men, students of a college, who were no anarchists but on the contrary detested anarchism, were heard to say that the conduct of the murderer was justifiable, as the victim was going to expose his co-conspirators to punishment by disclosing matters in violation of his promise to keep the secret. This was a most flagrant instance of perversion of moral judgment in those young men, who honestly believed that what they were saying was right. They ought to have known that in the first place, quite apart from the question whether the conduct of the victim was morally right or wrong, the murderer could have no justification or excuse for his act; and that in the second place, the moral perplexity of the approver's position was entirely of his own making, he having joined a conspiracy to commit crime and having promised to keep its doings secret, and those who were exposed to danger by his breach of promise could have no just ground of complaint, as his conduct only brought them to justice and exposed them to the punishment which they justly deserved.

The foregoing are only two instances out of many in which we may find honest and good men going wrong from obliquity of moral vision, who could have been kept straight by timely moral instruction.

If the necessity of Moral Education is recognized, the difficulty of our obtaining the ready aid of religion in its support by reason of the diversity of creeds prevailing in this country, should not make us feel that necessity any the less. And I would suggest with all the earnestness I can command, that every educational institution, whatever may be its rank and whatever may be the subject it teaches, should have some arrangement for imparting moral instruction. For all men from the lowest artisan to the highest leader of society should be good moral men in order to do well their respective parts in life, and Moral Education is therefore necessary for all.

The details of a scheme of Moral Education I shall not here dwell upon. All I purpose to do will be to offer a few general suggestions for planning such a scheme.

The first requisite in a scheme of Moral Education is a competent moral instructor, that is, *one who knows morality and practises morality, and who likes his work and loves his pupils.*

Morality is necessary not only to be known but also to be practised, and a teacher who teaches it but does not practise it himself, and who "recks not his own read," seldom proves a successful teacher. The well-known text of the Bhagavat, "The words of the gods should be followed but not always their acts," has given rise to much doubt and difficulty. It is quite true that every honest teacher has to say, "Do as I say but not always as I do," for imperfect man can never practise all that he professes; but it is only pupils in advanced stages that can appreciate the saying rightly. For boys and immature youths, a moral teacher of uncommon virtue is needed, for they will sooner imitate his acts than translate his words into action.

Then the moral teacher should be one who likes his work and loves his pupils. Unless he likes his work, he will not be able to devote himself to it with that untiring energy which is necessary for its success. And unless he loves his pupils and sympathizes with them, he will not be able to secure that willing attention and obedience to his advice and direction, which are necessary for the success of his teaching. There is a remarkable story about Mahammad's sympathetic spirit towards those who sought his advice, which I have told in another place, and which will bear repetition here.

A poor old man had a son very fond of sugar, and he found it hard to supply the young man with that article of luxury. He sought the advice of the Prophet to help him out of his difficulty, and was told to come again with his son after a fortnight. He did so, and Mahammed in a decisive tone commanded the son to give up sugar, pointing out to him, that though inconvenient, it was not impossible to do so, if he tried to reduce gradually the quantity of sugar he took. The father and son made their bow and took leave, but in a few moments the old man came back, and begging the Prophet's pardon, asked him why it was that he took a fortnight's time to give what was such a simple advice after all. The Prophet smiled and said, he himself was very fond of sugar, and he did not think it right to advise any of his followers to give it up before seeing whether he could do so himself. The story may or may not be authentic, but the lesson it teaches is invaluable, namely, that a teacher should not direct his pupils to do that which he himself cannot or does not do, and that it is only where a teacher directs his pupils to do that which he believes to be right and which he practises himself, that the lesson is imparted with real force and makes a ready and effective impression.

It will not be easy to find such teachers. But it will be enough if we can have one such teacher for each large school, and the time table so arranged that he can give moral instruction to each class at least once a week. For small Secondary Schools and for Primary Schools, one moral teacher may be appointed to take charge of two or three schools, and he should receive travelling allowance in addition to his salary.

If competent teachers form the first requisite in a scheme of Moral Education, qualified pupils are the next requisite. For if the pupil is not fit to receive the instruction given, it will be of little avail. My saying this however must not be taken to imply that it is only good students that can benefit by moral instruction. If that were so, Moral Education would be of little use. The truth is that every human being of sound mind is, or can be made, fit to receive moral instruction, if we take him step by step through its different stages from the simple to the more complex.

The fitness of a student for Moral Education is the effect of heredity and environments. Heredity we cannot change, environments we can; and by change of environments we can more or less counteract the effect of heredity. If heredity and environments have already fitted a student for a certain stage of Moral Education, we may begin from that stage. If they have not fitted him for any stage, we must begin from the beginning. And we should so adjust the environments of the student as to make him more and more fit for receiving moral instruction. We should begin with regulating his diet. The influence of food on temperament is not a mere superstitious fiction, but is a physiological fact. Meat diet and alcoholic drink should be prohibited for students in Indian climate. They are in this country as a rule not only unnecessary but injurious for the body and the mind. A student's food should be substantial but simple, strengthening but not stimulating.

The play and pastimes of students should be healthful and cheering, but should not be made stimulating by unhealthy keen competition for prize and success. Play under the influence of such violent stimulus is as bad for the body as it is for the mind. It loses its character as healthful exercise, produces over-exertion of the physical system and undue excitement of the selfish instincts, and may awaken jealousy and other unpleasant feelings in the unsuccessful competitors.

The text-books of students require careful regulation to make them helpful for Moral Education.

A large part of the world's attractive literature, which is the work of the vigorous infancy and adolescence of our race when men were prone to quarrel (they have not alas! improved much yet), in extolling patriotism and heroism, really teaches hatred and cruelty to our neighbours. A philosophical writer has aptly observed, the cult of love which Christianity teaches one day in the week in churches, is counteracted by the cult of hate which Greek and Latin literature teaches the other days of the week in schools and colleges. The same would be the fate of Moral Education imparted during the few brief hours spared for it, if we do not take care to prevent its salutary effect being counteracted by any unsalutary literature taught during the greater portion of the school-time. Happily our work here is easy. For besides what is taken exception to, all the great literatures of the world contain much that is unexceptionable, though unhappily (I feel bound to add) an idea is gaining ground that tame didactic pieces in literature are not suitable for boys, and that they require stirring narrative and descriptive pieces for their reading lessons. Let them have narrative and descriptive pieces by all means, in addition to those that are didactic, only let them not have pieces which stimulate selfish instincts too much, Literary works are not the only books open to objection. There are books on other subjects open to similar objection, such as popular books on science with a materialistic tendency calculated to lower our lofty ideals of life and human destiny. No one can take any just exception to professedly scientific or philosophic writings, merely by reason of their belonging to one or other school of thought, because in the first place, in the interests of truth and freedom of thought, the writings of every school deserve study, and because in the second place, they are addressed to mature minds capable of thinking for themselves. But the same thing cannot be said of popular books on science or philosophy which are meant for readers incapable of judging for themselves, which propound views implying that they are the only true views on the subjects dealt with, and which imperceptibly instil into untrained minds, ideas of debatable correctness and doubtful propriety.

The third requisite in a scheme of Moral Education is, a well arranged and well graduated syllabus of the course of instruction. I will not enter into the details of such a syllabus, but will only offer a few general suggestions as to the lines on which a syllabus of moral instruction should proceed.

The first point to bear in mind in drawing up a syllabus of moral instruction is, that morality is not only to be learnt but is also to be practised by the learner. The teacher should see that the principles taught are not merely learnt, but are readily accepted as true and willingly followed in practice by his pupils. They should be told each to be the watchman of his own conduct, and should be accustomed early to take pleasure in voluntarily doing what is right, and compulsion and punishment should be wholly excluded.

My next suggestion would be to avoid controversial matters, altogether in the early, and as far as possible also in the later, stages. At the commencement of a course of Moral Education, it will be enough to point out that there is a distinction between right and wrong just as there is between true and false, that the right is good and is immediately or in the long run a source of pleasure, and the wrong is bad and is immediately or in the long run a source of pain; and to illustrate these principles by simple and striking examples. A little later, the same principles should be illustrated by more complex examples, and the additional principle should be explained and illustrated, namely, that the converse is not always true, that is, that what is a source of pleasure is not always right.

From the commencement of the course of moral instruction, the nature of the good qualities, Veracity, Honesty, Temperance, Modesty, Fortitude, Forgiveness, and Benevolence, and of their opposites, Mendacity, Dishonesty, Intemperance, Pride, Cowardice, Vindictiveness, and Malevolence, and their effects upon the individual and upon society, should be gradually explained. And students should be asked to observe for themselves how far their own conduct is influenced by their good or bad qualities, and to try to improve day by day. Conduct registers are not of much use. Students should be asked to record their day's conduct before the day's end in the tablet of their memory, and to go to bed with a solemn resolve to mend the day's errors on the morrow. They should be told that the selfish instincts become unnecessary after the development of reason, and should be fully restrained by reason.

The aim of the moral teacher from the very beginning should be to encourage altruism and restrain egoism, and to inculcate devotion to duty with self-abnegation and without expectation of reward. This is a very high ideal no doubt; but unless we make our ideals very high, our realizations, which must fall short of our ideals, will be very low.

In thus asking moral teachers to fix very high ideals and to inculcate the principle of self-abnegation, I may be met by two or three objections which I ought to answer.

In the first place, some educationists say that it should be as futile to expect by Education to make a student excel in a virtue for which he does not by heredity possess the potentiality, as it would be to expect to make him attain the height of twenty or even ten feet by improving his environments. It is true that one cannot by Education acquire, or even excel in, any virtue for which the potentiality does not exist in him, but it is not true that a normal mind does not possess potentialities for all the ordinary virtues. Experience proves the contrary. For instances are not rare in which most surprising moral transformations for the better have been observed to take place under the influence of altered circumstances or earnest teachers.

In the second place, it is sometimes said that self-abnegation within certain limits may be good, but perfect self-abnegation, even if it was attainable, is not desirable. I deny this. So strong are the selfish instincts, that there is no fear of their being completely rooted out from any human heart and inaction or indifference to action following. They will remain there and continue to do their work for evil and partially also for good. The educator need not feel any anxiety lest they be rooted out, and he may direct his efforts entirely towards restraining them.

Tenderness towards our selfish instincts is the result of the dominance of material things in Western civilization, which has been brought about by, and which in its turn leads to, selfishness. In saying this, I fear I come face to face with an objection taken in no unkindly spirit by a friendly critic, who remarks unfavourably against a "tendency to compare Western materialism to its disadvantage with the assumed spirituality of the East." Now I do not claim spirituality as the monopoly of the East. But I do say that nurtured by a kind Nature, the East had less need to attend to self or the material side of the world, and had more time to think of not-self and of the spiritual world, while a less kind Nature forced the West to attend more to self and the material world, and left her less time to think of altruism and spirituality; and the result has been that while the East, with her less advanced material condition, has to look up to things spiritual for consolation and comfort, the material prosperity of the West binds her more and more to her attractive mundane things.

The only hope of liberation of the West from that bondage lies in her perception of the two great evils which her material prosperity has brought in its train, the fierce internal strife between labour and capital with its open strikes and riots and its secret anarchism, and the still more fierce external strife between nation and nation for gain and not for glory; and that deliverance of the West may come sooner if she views the peaceful poverty of the East with less supercilious eyes than she is accustomed to do, while the East may benefit by carefully observing what is going on in the West, with eyes not dazzled by her material splendour. But I must here stop, for I fear I have digressed too far, though I hope I have not been wholly irrelevant to my subject.

My last suggestion regarding Moral Education is, that moral instruction should not be considered as limited to the hours specially reserved for it, and to the text-books, if any, specially prescribed for it, but that there should be a direction to every teacher in every subject to avail himself of every opportunity afforded by lessons in his subject, to impress on students the morals they teach, and to note and correct gently every moral slip that a student may commit. We are each one of us in our conduct every day and every hour going through a course of moral exercises which require immediate correction.

IV. Religious Education. The problem of Religious Education is a difficult one, and its difficulty is enhanced in no small measure by the prevalence of a diversity of creeds in India. But if Religious Education is necessary, the difficulty of organizing a scheme of such education ought not to prevent us from doing our best to impart it.

If religion means the knowledge of a few irrational dogmas or the observance of a few unmeaning forms, then one may doubt the necessity of Religious Education. But if religion means, as in its proper sense it does mean, belief in an intelligent and infinite Being as the Creator and Governor of the Universe, belief in the immortality of the soul, and the moulding of life in a manner such as these beliefs require, then religion concerns not merely a part of man's life, but the whole of it, and Religious Education becomes more necessary than any other kind of Education. Moreover, morality, which we consider necessary, derives no small support from religion. For though in ordinary cases, the moral sense unaided by religious sentiment may enable us to distinguish between right and wrong, and the pleasurableness of righteous acts may suffice to induce us to do the right, yet in cases involving severe conflict of duties or serious sacrifice of interest, faith in an all-powerful beneficent moral Governor and in a future state of existence, seems to be the only guide of unswerving duty and the only refuge of suffering virtue.

Happily for us, notwithstanding the doubts entertained by a few European educationists, the religions of all great sects inhabiting India include the two beliefs and answer the general description of religion stated above. Religion understood in the above sense as meaning Natural Religion, that is, religion as it can be understood by the ordinary human mind unaided by revelation or inspiration, and as distingnished from Supernatural Religion, or religion revealed by supernatural process or apprehended by supernatural inspiration, can therefore be taught in schools and colleges without any serious difficulty arising from the existence of a diversity of creeds in the country.

Government has very wisely and justly adopted the policy of religious neutrality in this country, and nothing more than mere permissive action can be expected from it, that is, its leaving every educational institution free to make its own arrangements for imparting religious instruction, subject to two important conditions, namely, that no religious teacher should say anything that may give offence to the followers of any faith, and that religious instruction should be confined to doctrines and should not include rituals.

Subject to the above conditions, the authorities of every school or college should make their own arrangements for imparting religious instruction. The real difficulty here as in every other branch of Education is, to get a good teacher. And even when that difficulty is got over, the objection will still remain, that religious instruction that can be imparted on the foregoing plan, will be devoid of detail and therefore scanty and uninspiring, unless the teacher imparts into his teaching the particular doctrines of his own faith, which again will be open to the objection of his teaching a denominational and not a non-denominational religion. But these are objections unavoidable in the nature of things, and their force may be minimized by appointing as religious teachers persons of the same faith as the pupils to be taught.

In the case of students who are boarders of hostels attached to colleges, and whose daily life for the entire period of twenty-four hours is controlled by the authorities of their college and hostel, the necessity of making some provision for religious instruction and religious observance is imperative, and no college should insist upon students residing in its hostel if it cannot make such provision.

V. Female Education.

This includes every sort of education through all its stages, adapted to the requirements of females, supposing their requirements to be different in some respects from those of males. The organization of a scheme of Female Education is a head of my discourse which need not therefore detain me long. What I have said above about male education will apply to female education with only such modifications as the special requirements of females may render necessary.

One of these special requirements in my opinion is, that females should be taught in schools and colleges established exclusively for them, and provided as far as practicable with female teachers.

Another special requirement of female students is, that their curriculum should include subjects the study of which is calculated to impart knowledge or skill which will be useful to them in the management of their household, and in the discharge of those higher and more delicate duties which they may be called upon to perform as wife and as mother.

And regard being had to the circumstances of the country, and in particular to the backward state of Female Education, a third special requirement is, that the rules about attendance at lectures, and residence in hostels, should be relaxed in the case of female students as far as may be deemed reasonable.

VI. National Education.

National Education does not mean any particular sort of education, but means education of every sort through all its stages, adapted to the requirements of a nation. As a good deal of misconception, distrust, and odium attaches to what is called National Education in Bengal, a few words explaining its meaning may not be superfluous.

The National Education movement was started in connection with the agitation against the Partition of Bengal, but there were many that joined it as a purely educational movement, as the speeches at the inaugural meeting of the Bengal National Council of Education show. And the National Council of Education has all along worked as a purely educational body, and has kept the institutions under it wholly unconnected with politics. But the doings of students and teachers of a few schools which called themselves National Schools but were not connected with the National Council of Education, were viewed with suspicion and disapprobation by officials, who acting upon incorrect information extended their disfavour to the entire National Education movement. The object of the National Council of Education, as its memorandum of association will show, was to impart Education on national lines, not in opposition to but apart from, the existing system of Education.

The system of Education in every country the population of which belongs to one single nationality, must proceed on national lines, that is it must be adapted to the requirements of that nation. It is only in a country like India, inhabited by a diversity of races speaking different languages and following different creeds, but united under one rule, that the problem of Education presents a novel aspect. Here no common System of Education can be planned on any particular national lines; and the system that has been organized by Government or the Universities established by Government, is one that has been deemed best suited on the whole to meet the requirements of the different nations composing the population of the country. The medium of instruction that has been adopted (except for the earliest stages) is the language of the rulers, which all educated people have to learn, and which is understood by educated people all over the country. Religious Education has had to be left out in pursuance of the policy of religious neutrality wisely adopted by Government. And the system has generally been planned on the model of that prevailing in England which is the one that our rulers understand best, though it may not be the one best adapted to the requirements of the people of this country in many respects. There is ample scope therefore for the working of another system of Education side by side with the existing system, and framed on lines better adapted to the requirements of one particular race, the Bengalis, with such differences of adaptation for

Hindus and Mahomedans as their difference in creed may render necessary. And it is such a system that the Bengal National Council has been seeking to organize; and I may here parenthetically add, it is another similar system which the promoters of the Hindu University scheme have in view.

It may be said that Education which is the most potent agency for uniting the diverse races of men, should not be influenced by considerations of difference in nationality or religion, but should proceed on a cosmopolitan basis, and that every system of Education in the East should incorporate with it the best ideals of the West. That is true, but true only for the higher stages of Education. The assimilation of foreign ideals is desirable only in the later stages of mental growth. In the earlier stages it is not possible, and any attempt to force it on, will retard instead of accelarating the healthy development of the mind. Every student when commencing his Education brings with him in addition to his outfit of language, his stock of thoughts and sentiments, the gift of his nation, which the teacher, instead of ignoring and hastily displacing, should try to utilize and gradually improve. Want of due regard for this principle is, I think, the cause of some of those unsatisfactory results of English Education of which we hear so often. Some educationists think that these unsatisfactory results will disappear if English Education can be made more completely to fill the Indian mind, and that the remedy for all the defects of Education in India lies in transplanting the English system of Education more completely in this country. That is an erroneous view.

A learned historian of English Literature has remarked that Milton with his deep erudition has made Adam come to Paradise *via* England, and has made him 'act and talk as an English householder and an old Oxford man'. Some of our learned teachers from Oxford and Cambridge feel unhappy if they find any of Adam's descendants any where acting and talking differently from members of an English household and under-graduates of Oxford or Cambridge. The English student has many virtues, but he has his failings too. The Bengali student may have many failings, but he has his virtues too. Any attempt to transform the one into the other will be worse than futile. You may easily displace the virtues of the one, but you cannot easily replace them by the virtues of the other. The Bengali student should remain a Bengali and try to improve, but he should not attempt to imitate his English compeer.

That Education on national lines, that is, Education adapted to the national mental constitution of the student, is more advantageous than Education on foreign lines, may be shown by a comparison of elementary text-books written for English boys with those written for Bengali boys. In elementary books on Arithmetic and Geometry written for English boys, authors take great pains to illustrate by numerous concrete examples simple things which a Bengali boy does not feel much difficulty in understanding without the help of any such illustrations. To him the illustrations appear unnecessary and tedious, and for him they are waste of time and energy. It may be that the Bengali boy shows greater intelligence in the earlier than in the later stages of his career. If that be so, the teacher should reserve the profusion of his explanation for the later stages.

So also books like "Legends of Greece and Rome" and "Animal Story Book" which may interest English boys, and are for that reason sometimes recommended for Bengali boys, appear to the latter insipid and uninteresting. Books of a little more serious nature would be more suitable for them.

The hostel system which is considered so beneficial to English students, is, apart from religious and caste difficulties, not quite suitable for Hindu students. English educationists are sometimes heard to say that a residential college cannot be foreign to Hindu sentiment, as it had its counterpart in residence with the preceptor in ancient India. This is quite a mistaken view. There is no real analogy between residence in the preceptor's house in ancient India and residence in the college hostel at the present day. In the former case, what the pupil received from the preceptor was a gift of love which was next only to parental love, and what the preceptor got from the pupil in return was veneration which was next only to veneration for God; while in the latter case what the student receives and the college gives, the one receives and the other gives for money. And it should be borne in mind that the old Hindu sentiment against demand of money in return for training, which is allied to if not much stronger than the similar sentiment of Plato against the Sophists, still retains its sway notwithstanding the sweeping changes that have come upon society.

Then there is the language difficulty which can hardly be overrated. Indian students have to acquire knowledge through the medium of a difficult foreign language, and this not only overtaxes their energies but also cramps their thoughts. If a system of Education can be organized in which English is read as a second language, and other subjects are taught in the student's vernacular, he will learn these latter with greater ease, and will therefore learn English better than under our present system, as he will be able to spare more time and energy for its study.

The foregoing are only some of the many considerations which show that Education on national lines has ample scope for work, and there is reasonable expectation of its efficient work, side by side with the existing system. The field of such work will be limited within the range of each distinct nationality, but its efficacy will increase in proportion to the reduction of its area. Government cannot properly be asked to lend pecuniary aid to any such exclusively national system of Education, but it may justly be asked to lend its moral support and extend its patronization to such system. The Bengal National Council of Education, which has been working on the lines indicated above, should not be allowed to languish for want of support. It deserves encouragement from Government and from every well-wisher of the country.

CHAPTER V.

IMPARTING OF EDUCATION.

INSTRUMENTS OF EDUCATION.

I come now to the fifth division of my discourse, namely, Imparting of Education including Instruments of Education.

The remarks appropriate to this division of the subject may, for the sake of convenience, be arranged under the following heads :—

I. Teachers and Professors.

II. Inspectors and Directors.

III. Schools, Colleges, and Universities.

IV. Medium of Instruction and Text-Books.

V. Methods of Imparting Education

I. Teachers and Professors.

A teacher should be qualified for his work, intellectually, physically, and morally. He should know the subject he has to teach, know how to teach it, and know other allied subjects which throw light on the subject he teaches. He should possess a keen sense of sight and hearing to enable him to see and hear what his pupils are doing and saying, and a clear and powerful voice to make himself heard and understood by his pupils. And he should have liking for his work so that he may not feel tired soon ; he should have love for his pupils so that he may not be annoyed with them easily ; and he should have a high character that he may command the respect and attention of his pupils. All this is easily seen, and will be readily admitted. The difficulty lies in finding such teachers ; and even when such teachers are found, very few employers including Government will be found ready to pay the remuneration necessary to obtain their services.

Every one who knows a subject may not know how to teach it; but one who knows a subject well and is possessed of bright intelligence, may be expected to know how to teach it. Intellectual fitness of a teacher may therefore be proved by high academic distinction. His physical fitness may be easily tested. And for proof of his moral fitness, we must depend upon certificates of character.

The Degree in Teaching, namely, Bachelor of Teaching, which has been recently instituted, and which is obtainable after special training in the science and art of Teaching for a certain time, may be taken as a substitute for some of the above mentioned tests of fitness. As things stand at present, the degree in Teaching may be accepted as a test of intellectual fitness only. But the Regulations for that degree may be so modified as to make the degree a test of physical and moral fitness also.

If the Regulations for the degree of Bachelor of Teaching provide that no student shall be admitted to a Training College for Teachers unless his physical fitness is proved by suitable tests, and his moral fitness is certified to by special testimonials, and that no one shall be sent up for the examination for the degree unless he has shown steady, diligent, careful, and intelligent work during his period of training, the B. T. degree will be a test of intellectual, physical, and moral fitness. And I would suggest that the B. T. Regulations should be modified in the manner indicated.

This suggestion may be objected to on the ground that it would make the B. T. Regulations uncommonly stringent. My answer is that that is but just proper, as the work which a candidate for the B. T. degree is preparing himself for, is uncommonly important, and the responsibility he will have to undertake is uncommonly great. The training which one should receive for training others, ought to be uncommonly strict and efficient.

But these suggested changes in the Regulations will hardly be just, and can hardly be expected to produce their desired effect, unless two other changes are simultaneously made, namely, change in the scale of salary for teachers to make the Education Service more attractive, and change in the teaching staff of Training Colleges to make those colleges more efficient.

If the highly inadequate salaries which teachers now get, are all that our Bachelors of Teaching can expect, it will not be just to subject them during their period of training to more stringent conditions than those now in force; nor can we expect any large number of brilliant graduates to be likely to join the Teaching profession with its present discouraging prospects. Then again, the few brilliant graduates who, through adverse circumstances such as their anticipated inability from poverty to maintain themselves during the period of early struggle in the professions of Law and Medicine, may be driven to join the Teaching profession, will not be able to devote all their energy to their work as teachers. With the continual rise in the expense of living, they are obliged to undertake the work of private tuition to earn something wherewith to supplement their small salaries in order to meet their necessary expense, so that they can have neither spare time nor spare energy to prepare properly for their work as school teachers. They have often to work as private tutors from 7 to 9 o'clock in the morning, then hurry home, take a hurried meal, and hasten to school where they are just in time but quite out of breath, and unfit to take up their school work immediately. Nor have they any near prospect of promotion to stimulate their energy and create any enthusiasm for their work amidst these unfavourable circumstances.

What I have just said applies to schools whether under Government or under private management, and the picture I have presented is not at all overdrawn, as every one who has any experience in the matter will be able to say. This is a deplorable state of things, and we can hardly expect any educational reform to be effective, unless the pay and prospects of teachers are improved. Improved modes of teaching, improved schemes of study, and improved methods of inspection, may be helpful to good teachers; but it is teachers who have to do the work primarily, and if we cannot get good teachers to begin with, and if our teachers feel no inducement to work with whole hearted devotion, no real improvement in Education can be effected.

If the state of things in Government institutions is bad, in private schools it is worse. Very few of these latter have any endowments in their support, they have to rely mainly on the schooling fees realized from students, and the poverty of the people prevents these fees being raised high; so they naturally endeavour to keep their scale of salaries below that fixed by Government. If Government raises its scale of salaries, as it can do and ought to do, that will have a beneficial effect all round. For as the scale fixed by Government is taken for the standard, if that is raised, teachers of private schools will feel justified in demanding increased salaries, and the authorities of those schools will feel bound to comply with that demand, and to raise schooling fees if need be. The result will be improvement in the quality of Education bought at some sacrifice of its quantity. For some of the small schools in poor localities will not be able to meet the increased demand upon them, and will in consequence have to be closed. And the question then arises, how far should salaries of teachers be raised, so as to secure appreciable improvement in the quality of Education without leading to any very considerable reduction in its quantity. It is neither feasible nor will it be deemed desirable to raise the salary scale so high as would lead to the closing of half the number of our schools. The improved Education of one half of the present school going population will hardly be accepted as adequate compensation against the other half being deprived of Education. The question, as I have already remarked in another place, resembles one of the class known as maxima minima problems, and what we have to determine is, the extent to which the salaries of teachers may be raised, so that the resulting improvement in Education may be a maximum, regard being had to the increase in its efficiency as well as to the decrease in its area. Maxima minima problems in Mathematics admit of solution when the necessary data are definitely given. Here the data are indefinite, and all that can be done is to proceed tentatively, gradually, and cautiously. I would accordingly suggest that regard being had to the present scale of salaries, it be raised not less than 25, but not more than 50 per cent, along with a similar raising of the scale of schooling fees where necessary. And I would further suggest that no one should be appointed as a teacher who does not intend to stick to the Teaching profession at least for some reasonable time.

The other change I have already referred to, is, increase in the efficiency of Colleges for the training of teachers. The instructive staff of these Colleges should consist of men of superior ability and attainments fit to train those that will have to train others. They should be men thoroughly well versed in the theory and practice of Teaching, possessed of ripe experience specially of Indian students and their educational needs, and possessed also of mature judgment and discrimination to enable them to adapt and apply general principles to particular cases instead of blindly following them in every case. This last mentioned qualification is all the more necessary, seeing that Education is still an art and not a science, that educational theories are diverse and conflicting, and that text-books on Education, though otherwise good, are often found to make hasty generalizations and to lay down rules the correctness of which has been but imperfectly tested. Young graduates in Teaching fresh from college, like young Medical practitioners, are apt to have implicit faith in all that is said in their text-books; and it is only after long experience that they find that their faith was misplaced, and that actual cases are more varied in their nature than rules laid down in books can provide for.

What I have said about Teachers will apply to Professors, with the exception of the remarks about the B. T. degree which is not necessary for the latter. But there are two additional matters relating to Professors which require special notice, namely, (1) the division of professors into two classes, members of the Indian Education Service and members of the Provincial Education Service, and (2) the relation of Indian students to European professors.

Regarding the first mentioned matter, I have already said what I have to say in an early part of this discourse under the head of General Principles. I need not repeat all that, but I shall only add that this arrangement, which is incompatible with British justice, should be modified without delay, and professors should be classified, and their pay, privileges, and rank regulated, according to their intrinsic merits, and irrespective of all extrinsic circumstances, subject to one qualification, namely, the grant of a special allowance to European professors for serving in a distant country.

. . . .

The second matter is one of considerable delicacy, and fain would I have left it untouched, were it not for its great and growing importance.

Fifty years ago, the relation of Indian students to European professors was all that could be desired. European professors treated their Indian pupils with kindness, and when occasion arose for severity of treatment, it was loving severity. And their pupils in return showed them affectionate reverence. But unhappily, the state of things is now somewhat different.

In saying this, I do not lose sight of the bright examples we still have of very kind and sympathetic European professors among the senior and also the junior members of the Education service. Two instances come prominently before me. One is that of the head of the first College in Bengal, who would do honour to any educational office. He is so kind to Indian students, that on one occasion he warmly interceded on their behalf with one of their own countrymen who as chairman of a meeting had expressed dissatisfaction at their rowdy behaviour. The other instance is that of a young professor of Economics, who had won the love and esteem of his pupils, but who unhappily for them has been transferred to another department of the public service. I should add that most of the European professors of Missionary Colleges also are still of the old type. But though that is so, I regret to say that the relation between European professors and Indian pupils is not altogether as happy as it should be. Perhaps the fault lies on both sides; or perhaps it would be more correct to say, if we view the matter with philosophic composure and optimistic complacence, that no great blame attaches to either side, and that the unhappy state of things is the temporary result of certain causes which have been in operation during the stage of transition through which we have been passing, but it will cease with the cessation of those causes as soon as we settle down.

With spread of Education and freedom of the press, two great gifts of England to India, educated Indians have been competing successfully with Englishmen, and have been criticising the conduct of Englishmen in various fields, and are agitating fearlessly for privileges of various sorts. This state of things, though viewed with proud satisfaction by all noble minded Englishmen, is, as is but natural, looked upon with strong resentment and petty jealousy by inferior men. Again, the recent renascence of the East has caused some uneasiness to the West, and given rise to the false doctrine of antagonism between the White Race and the Coloured Races. And the Hindus of Bengal whose language unquestionably belongs to the Aryan family, and who were formerly regarded as a branch of the Aryan race, are now supposed by ethnologists to be of the Mongolo-Dravidian type. The result of all this has been the evoking of a latent sub-conscious feeling of contempt in the European mind for the Indians as an inferior race of men. It is perhaps the existence of this feeling which sometimes produces strained relations between Englishmen and Indians. Though culture "hates hatred," even cultured minds here have not always been proof against it, and sad to say, that unhallowed feeling has made incursions within the sacred precincts of the temple of learning itself. If any latent feeling of contempt exists, it will manifest itself in many offensive ways. Where a European professor has contempt for his Indian pupil, the latter will feel it, and, though extremely wrong, will not unfrequently resent it. And the result will be most lamentable. In the first place, the existence of such a feeling in the professor will prevent him from exerting himself to make his teaching successful, as he will believe the ill success of his teaching to be ascribable not to his own inefficiency but to the inferiority of his pupil. In the second place, it will prevent his teaching being effective as it will be received by his pupil in a repellent and not in a receptive attitude of mind. But happily through the moral influence of certain sympathetic officials (notably that of the President of the University Institute and of the Principal of the Presidency College) a change for the better is already evident.

And I firmly trust that with the growing appreciation of the real merits of Indians by Englishmen and of Englishmen by Indians a happy state of things will soon be brought about.

II. Inspectors and Directors.

Inspectors are needed to supervise and guide the work of teaching. But we must have good teachers to begin with. For it is they who have to do the work of teaching. Some supervision is good for the teacher as furnishing him with a motive to do his work well, and some guidance from an officer of greater learning and experience is helpful to him in correcting his errors. But too much supervision and too much guidance involve waste of time, energy, and money, and also prove embarrassing instead of being helpful. And any money that may be saved by reducing the numerical strength of the inspecting agency within proper limits, may be usefully spent in improving the teaching staff by raising the salary of teachers.

If with our limited funds, we can increase the strength of the teaching agency only by reducing that of the agency for inspection, the question how far the one may be reduced for improving the other, so as to give a maximum of efficiency in the result, is a maxima minima problem the solution of which is not very easy. We must proceed tentatively and cautiously; and all that an outsider without the help of detailed facts and figures can venture to suggest would be, that the numerical strength of the inspecting agency should be just sufficient for the inspection of every school at least once but not more than twice in a year. And I need hardly add that the inspecting agency should be composed of men of much greater ability, learning, and experience, than those whose work they have to inspect.

Directors are necessary to co-ordinate the work of their respective provinces, and the only suggestion I have to make regarding the office of Director is that it should be held by an educationist of mature Indian experience.

III. Schools, Colleges, and Universities.

Schools. Bengali students have to work in an insalubrious climate, and have to work hard in acquiring knowledge through the medium of a difficult foreign language. So their health is to be particularly attended to. We must therefore insist upon the sanitary requirements of school buildings being strictly fulfilled. School rooms should be dry, should have free access of light and air, and should be neat and clean. Every school should have sufficient play ground attached to it, and if possible, a small garden and some land for showing by experiment the growth of plants. But considering the poverty of the country, we must not demand anything in the nature of architectural elegance.

It should be well understood that it is part of the teacher's duty to make his pupils learn and practise the lesson that the school house and school furniture should be used with care and kept neat and clean. This lesson is as useful as any other lesson that a boy learns at school.

The teaching staff should be competent and adequate, and every teacher should have at least an hour free from class teaching every day, to devote to the correction of written exercises or other similar work.

The last three or at least the last two teachers should be o equal ability and consequently of equal rank and salary, with the teacher immediately above them, so that the lowest classes may be properly taught. It is a great mistake to neglect the teaching of these classes, as is often the case, in the vain hope that the deficiency may be made up in the higher classes. It is in the lowest classes that the first bent is given to the infant mind, and any wrong notion there imbibed, any mispronunciation there learnt, or any bad method of writing there practised, becomes difficult to get rid of afterwards. Education will be made much easier if we can go on learning only as we proceed, instead of having to unlearn much that has been laboriously learnt in the earlier stages of our progress.

Another suggestion which I have to make with reference to the teaching staff of a school, is, that every class below the third should be placed in the sole charge of one teacher who will teach all the subjects except the classical language (Sanskrit or Arabic or Persian) for which a separate teacher will generally be found necessary. One advantage of this arrangement (and an advantage of great value in the training of little boys) will be that the pupils will feel the personal influence of the teacher and the teacher will feel a personal interest in his pupils, much more than can be expected if each class is taught by a number of teachers, and each teacher has to teach a number of classes.

Another advantage of this arrangement will be that it will create in each teacher a wholesome emulation to make his class the best in the school.

Nor will there be any difficulty in carrying out such an arrangement. In the first three classes it may perhaps be desirable to have each subject taught by a teacher who has specialized in it; but for the other classes, every teacher ought to be able to teach all the subjects usually taught (except the classical languages). If he is not able to do so, he is not fit to be appointed a teacher. Every teacher ought to have a general knowledge of the different subjects usually taught in a school so as to be able to teach the classes below the first three.

Colleges. The transition from School to College is quite naturally regarded as an important point in the educational career of a student. When a student after finishing his School course and passing his Matriculation Examination is ready to enter College, he may be supposed to have attained maturity of intellect sufficient to enable him to take care of himself, and to prosecute his further study with only such help as he may get from his professors at college, and without the aid of any private tutor at home. In attaining that standard of progress he must also, quite apart from any University rules, attain a certain age ranging ordinarily between fourteen and seventeen years. According to the advocates of the residential system of collegiate Education, there is another important change in the students environments, namely, change from home life to hostel life. But that is a conventional and an arbitrary and not a natural and necessary change, as the residential system is not a universal and necessary adjunct of College Education. The standard of attainment at the end of the School course is also a matter of convention, and cannot be fixed for all time, but must advance with the progress of human knowledge. Some educationists think that the first two years of our present College course should be transferred to the School course, and students should be detained at School for a further period of two years, that is, up to the age of eighteen. That is not a correct view. If the College course up to the B. A. standard is to remain a four years course as at present, with an M. A. course of two years, and with a B. L. course of three years, no one will be able to obtain the M. A. degree before he is twenty-four, and to obtain the B. L. degree before he is twenty-five, That will never do, for life especially within the tropics is too short for all that. If it is intended to reduce the B. A. course to one of two years time, that difficulty will not arise, but there will still remain a serious practical difficulty to meet, as very few of our schools will be able to teach what is now taught in the first two years at college. So that College Education must for some time at least continue to commence at the point at which it now begins.

Nor is it desirable that a college should be exclusively residential. No student should be compelled to reside in the college hostel if he can attend college from his home. Home, notwithstanding all its disadvantages, has important advantages which no college hostel can give, and home life has a disciplinary effect which can hardly be over-estimated. It is not the college hostel with its mechanical uniformity of comfortable routine, but the home with its variations of comfort and discomfort and occasional distraction, that can form the proper training ground for preparing men for the world. And the discomfort which some young English professors fresh from their residential colleges, feel amidst their Indian pupils with their uncouth manners, would go to show that hostel life creates exclusiveness, and is not conducive to the growth of that cosmopolitan spirit which can easily adapt itself to its surroundings.

For students who cannot attend college from their homes, some residential arrangement is necessary; but even in their case the hostel system is not the best. The mess system, in which students live under supervision of their college authorities but manage their own affairs themselves in houses provided for them at reasonable rent by their colleges, is much better calculated to train young men for the world outside the college walls.

There are two matters relating to colleges which call for some remarks, namely, the question of fees, and the question of attendance at lectures.

The college fees should not be raised, as some educationsts recommend, for the purpose of making Education expensive so as to stop overcrowding in colleges by preventing poor people from seeking admission. That would not be just, for Education is not a luxury to be confined to the rich. The proper limit to which college fees may be raised is that which is required to enable unendowed colleges to maintain themselves on an efficient footing. That limit will depend upon the scale of salaries of professors and the expenses of equipment of the college.

The question of attendance at lectures is an important one, and there is great difference of opinion upon the point. The existing Regulations of the Calcutta University require a student to attend 75 per cent of the lectures in each subject, in order to entitle him to a certificate that he has prosecuted a regular course of study in that subject.

While fully appreciating the value of training received from a competent teacher, and of steady application to study, I am unable to support the present system, which seeks to obtain by the operation of compulsory mechanical rules that which can be secured only by voluntary intelligent work. The present rule may compel a student to be present at lectures which he does not find instructive, either by reason of their intrinsic defect or by reason of his knowing the subject of the lectures sufficiently well, so that he might have employed his time better than by attending the lectures. The rule therefore in such cases entails waste of time. This is the first objection to the rule. Again the rule by always securing a well attended class for the lecturer, often prevents him from knowing whether his lectures are proving really useful to his pupils or not, and deprives him of the incentive he would otherwise have had, to put forth all his energy in making his lectures useful and attractive in order to secure a full class. The rule therefore indirectly operates against encouraging efficiency. This is the second objection to the rule.

Then again, the rule imposes an exceedingly heavy burden of unnecessary work on professors, on the clerical staff of colleges, and on the University. The roll has to be called for every hour, that is for every period of lecture on each subject, and this with a class usually consisting of between 100 and 150 students, must reduce the time of lecture and exhaust the energy of the lecturer by an appreciable amount. At the time of sending to the University applications from candidates for examination, the amount of arithmetical and clerical work to be done by the clerks of every fairly large college is something trying. And the number of hard and exceptional cases in which applications for special consideration are sent by the colleges to the Syndicate and by the Syndicate to Senate under the Regulations, impose a large amount of heavy work on the college staff and on the Syndicate and the Senate. The rule therefore involves a great waste of time and energy which might otherwise have been more profitably employed. This is the third objection to the rule.

Then it has to be admitted with regret that the rule, which is very stringent in its operation, and under which learned members of the Senate press for exclusion from examination of candidates even where their cases have been recommended by the Syndicate for favourable consideration, leads unscrupulous students, of whom there are always a few among a large number, to have recourse to unfair practice which may go undetected when the classes are large.

On the other hand, if we have no such rule, and if the lectures are really instructive, college students who are young men of judgment and intelligence and who may be assumed to understand their own interest, will not wilfully absent themselves from lectures. A few bad students may not attend lectures if there is no compulsory rule, but if they attend under compulsion, it does them little good, and they only crowd the lecture room to the inconvenience of others.

This is a sound common sense view of the matter, and is the view adopted by most of the great Universities of Great Britain.

I would therefore venture to suggest that the rule about compulsory attendance be abrogated, and certificates of general conduct from heads of affiliated colleges be accepted as sufficient evidence of students having prosecuted a regular course of study without any specification relating to attendance at lectures.

Universities.

I come now to the consideration of Universities. Much might be said under this head. I shall confine my remarks and suggestions to the following matters, namely, (1) Office of Vice-Chancellor, (2) Constitution of the Syndicate, (3) Constitution of a Faculty of Agriculture, (4) Teaching by the University, (5) Regulations of the University.

(1) *Office of Vice-Chancellor.* One important question relating to the Office of Vice-Chancellor is. whether it should be an honorary or a salaried office. Some maintain that it should continue to be honorary as heretofore, others say that it ought to be salaried. There are cogent considerations in favour of both views.

We have hitherto had only honorary Vice-Chancellors and they have on the whole done well. As honorary Vice-Chancellors, we can have high officials or recognized non-official leaders of the public, whose position adds to the dignity of the University and commands respect. And even when they are not of very high official or non-official rank, the mere fact of their serving without pay invests them with a natural dignity, and secures for them respect from every one. But on the other hand, the work of the University has grown so heavy and exacting, that it is very difficult to find any honorary worker for the office of Vice-Chancellor, and it has now become a matter of almost absolute necessity to appoint paid Vice-Chancellors. If it be absolutely neeessary to appoint a paid Vice-Chancellor, I would suggest that the pay should not be less than that of one of the principal Secretaries to Government, so that the services of really competent men may be secured and the dignity of the office may continue unimpaired.

(2) *Constitution of the Syndicate.* The most important question connected with the Constitution of the Syndicate is, whether the majority of the Syndicate should always be composed of members of the educational service, public and private. The Universities Act (VIII of 1904), following the recommendation of the majority of the Indian Universities Commission, has answered that question in the affirmative (see section 15 of the Act). I dissented from that recommendation and I still retain the view I then expressed in my Note of Dissent. I entertain this view not because I am wanting in sympathy with the teaching profession or in appreciation of its services—I was at one time an humble member of that noble profession—but because I think that considering that the Syndicate has often to sit in judgment on the acts and work of teachers, teachers should not form a majority of the Syndicate merely by reason of their being teachers. But they may well form a majority of the Syndicate by reason of their ability, attainments and character entitling them to the confidence of the Senate and the public. To secure this result we do not require any rule controlling election to the Syndicate. If the electorates, that is the Faculties and the Senate, are composed of members who are alive to the true

interests of Education, and the Education service public and private is not wanting in members answering the above description and willing to serve on the Syndicate, there will be a majority and more than a bare majority of teachers on that body. As I hope and trust that that will always be the case, I will not quarrel with the statutory rule of majority as it now stands. But I feel bound to note with regret the fact that even that statutory rule has failed to give satisfaction to some of those in whose interest it has been made. Perhaps they wish the Syndicate to be composed not merely of a majority, but exclusively, of teachers, and it is they who often show want of confidence in the Syndicate, as will be seen from the proceedings of the Senate before which recommendations of the Syndicate are opposed not unfrequently by members of the Teaching profession.

(3) *Constitution of a Faculty of Agriculture.* I have already (see p. 101) given my reasons for suggesting the constitution of aFaculty of Agriculture, and I need not repeat them. I only refer to that suggestion once again in its proper place here.

(4) *Teaching by the University.* This is a very important matter, and in connection with it, much misconception exists.

When the Calcutta University was established, it was regarded as an examining and a teaching University. That was true in this sense, that it did not teach directly, but it regulated and controlled teaching by prescribing courses of study and even text-books for its examinations, and making study in its affiliated colleges a condition precedent to admission to its examinations. The present Act (VIII of 1904) and the Regulations made under it, make provision for direct teaching by our Universities while retaining the provisions for teaching by affiliated colleges, and the question arises, how to adjust teaching by the University with teaching by its affiliated Colleges. And that again raises a prior question, what is the true meaning of a Teaching University.

If a single College constitutes a University which examines the students of that college and confers degrees on them, that is a teaching and also an examining University of the simplest type involving no discordant elements. If again the federation of a number of Colleges constitutes a University, then too, it is a teaching as well as an examining University, the constituent colleges as distinct units forming its teaching agency, and their combination forming its examining agency. And the difference between such a University and the University of Calcutta as it was under its former Act, is this, that while in the former case it is the colleges that constitute the University, in the latter case the University has an independent existence as a separate body, and the affiliated colleges are altogether distinct from it, so that teaching by the affiliated colleges, though controlled by, cannot be regarded as identical with, teaching by the University, in the same way as teaching by the federated colleges can be regarded as teaching by the University which their federation constitutes. The constitution of such a teaching University also, though somewhat complex, involves no incompatible elements. But the Calcutta University under the present Act and Regulations, with its direct teaching agency and with its affiliated Colleges as teaching agencies of the same grade, is a Teaching University of a supler-complex type involving elements not quite easy to harmonize.

If a Teaching University means a University that teaches directly and systematically, the Calcutta University can be called a Teaching University only as regards Law. And even there, it is not a purely Teaching University, being a Teaching University as regards its own Law College, and an Examining University in regard to its affiliated Law Colleges. Then as regards Arts and Science, it cannot be called a Teaching University, as it has no arrangement for systematic teaching of Arts or Science, though it has some professors and lectures to teach some Arts subjects, and may soon have some professors to teach some Science subjects. And the real difficulty arises from its taking in hand the work of teachlng the same subjects up to the same standard, that is done by its affiliated Colleges. The University regulates and controls the teaching work of its affiliated Colleges, but who is to regulate and control the teaching work of its own professors and its own Colleges? This state of things must place the affiliated Colleges at a disadvantage when competing with the University Colleges. With human imperfections, it will be difficult to prevent injustice being done in some cases, and it will be still more difficult to prevent the impression being created that justice is not done in all cases.

There are only two possible ways of meeting this difficulty. One is to have no University teaching which competes with the teaching in any affiliated College, and the other is to place University Colleges and University professors on exactly the same footing as affiliated Colleges and their professors. The former course will not be practicable, because on the one hand some of the affiliated Colleges, such as the Presidency College, are able and willing to teach all subjects up to the highest standard, and it is not desirable to prevent their so doing, so that competition cannot be avoided by confining University teaching to the post graduate stage; and because on the other hand, the affiliated Colleges are found unable to make room for all students, and the University must therefore provide for the teaching of those students who cannot obtain admission in its affiliated Colleges. The only course left open therefore is to prevent unequal competition by placing University Colleges and University professors on the same footing as affiliated Colleges and their professors. And for that purpose it is necessary to exclude from the governing body of a University College, not only the Vice-Chancellor who under existing arrangements is the ex-officio president, but all members of the Syndicate as well.

The only practical suggestion therefore that I can make will be, that the course indicated above should be scrupulously followed.

(5) *Regulations of the University.*

I have offered suggestions for amending or altering particular Regulations of the Calcutta University as occasion arose in the course of the preceding discussion. All I propose to do here is to consider them generally, and to make one general suggestion regarding them, which experience of their operation for more than five years has shown to be necessary.

My suggestion is for revision of the Regulations as a body, for the purpose of simplifying them.

Some of the Regulations, by reason of their complexity, entail in their operation expenditure of an amount of time and energy for which the advantage supposed to be gained by such complex rules is hardly a sufficient compensation. To give one instance out of many, take the Regulation relating to the minimum pass marks in English for the Matriculation Examination to which I have already referred (see p. 12). About ten thousand candidates appear at that examination, and the amount of time required in tabulating marks and making out the pass list according to that complicated Regulation is something considerable, and that circumstance delays the publication of the result of the examination by quite an appreciable interval. But the possible advantage gained is but slight, and it will not matter much if we make 72 marks as the minimum pass marks in English in all cases, instead of limiting the adoption of that minimum to cases where a candidate obtains

40 marks in one of the papers. Take again the rules relating to attendance at lectures. In order that a deficiency in the required percentage by even a small fraction may be dispensed with, the case must come first before the Syndicate and then (if the Syndicate is in favour of the student) before the Senate, thereby entailing no small expenditure of time, whereas it would have been enough if the rules had left the dispensing power in the hands of the College authorities with suitable definition of a regular course of study.

I am fully alive to the necessity of amplified language and detailed provision in our rules, to prevent ambiguity and to meet possible contingencies. But amplified language and detailed provisions, if they help us in one direction, prove the reverse of helpful in another. Superfluous language becomes itself a source of ambiguity, and complex provisions, though they may not succeed in meeting all possible contingencies, are sure to entail loss of time in their application to cases coming within their scope. Very simple rules will not meet the requirements of the complicated concerns of modern society. Nor will very complex rules which entail loss of time in their application, meet the requirements of the present day when we are living under high pressure, and when time is so precious. We must avoid extremes and keep to the golden mean which our University Regulations have failed to observe.

IV. Medium of Instruction.

The important question under this head is, whether English or the student's Vernacular should form the medium of instruction. Some maintain that it should be the Vernacular, while others contend that it should be English. It is not necessary to consider the early history of the question, which was discussed with great warmth immediately after the establishment of British rule in India. It will be enough to discuss it with reference to present conditions. I have already had occasion to consider this question in connection with another head of my discourse, namely, Organisation of a System of Education (see p. 64.) and I refer to it again because it comes here also in its proper place. I shall deal with it very briefly, noticing points which have not been touched upon before ; but some repetition of what has already been said will be unavoidable in order to preserve continuity of argument. This will, I hope, be excused, considering the great importance of the question.

There are reasons for and against the two conflicting views, and they may be summed up thus. On the one hand, the vernacular is learnt without any conscious effort to learn it, and what is taught through the medium of the vernacular is learnt with greater ease, understood with greater thoroughness, and retained with greater tenacity, than knowledge imparted through the medium of English which itself has to be learnt with considerable effort, and is not always easily understood, so that it is more convenient to make the learner's vernacular the medium of instruction ; but on the other hand, as English has to be learnt by every Indian student not only for learning the higher branches of knowledge in which vernacular text-books are not available, but also for holding communication with the ruling class, and as there is great diversity of vernaculars in India and even in any one Province like Bengal, while English is understood more or less all over the country, it would tend to ultimate convenience to adopt English as the medium.

Weighing these conflicting considerations against each other, I think the correct answer to the question is, to make the student's Vernacular the medium of instruction up to the Matriculation Examination standard, English being read as a second language, and to make English the sole medium in the Collegiate stage.

There are two objections to this course,—first, that it is not practicable, and second, that even if practicable, it is not desirable, as it will retard the progress of High Education—which ought to be met.

With reference to the Primary stage of Education, there cannot be any difference of opinion. The objections relate to the Secondary stage. It is said that there are no good text-books in all the Indian vernaculars in the different subjects of the Matriculation Examination, nor are there good teachers who can teach those subjects in the different vernaculars, nor again will it be easy for the University to find examiners in all the subjects who are competent to examine answers given in the different vernaculars in use within its jurisdiction.

It cannot be denied that the difficulty arising from one or more of the three wants, namely, want of good text-books, want of good teachers, and want of good examiners, does exist. The rule for making the student's vernacular the medium of instruction in the Secondary stage can therefore be made compulsory only where practicable, it being declared to be simply permissive in all other cases. A permissive rule of this kind in the subject of History is already in operation in the Calcutta University, as regards the Indian vernaculars, Bengali, Hindi, Uriya, Assamese, and Urdu, and it has caused no difficulty. I would suggest that the rule may be extended to the other subjects for the Matriculation Examination other than languages. There are good text-books in some of those subjects in some if not all the vernaculars named above, and good text-books in the other subjects and in the other languages will soon be forthcoming if the rule is promulgated. Competent teachers and examiners will also be available from among graduates whose vernaculars those languages are, or who have specially studied those vernaculars.

There still remains a particular aspect of the objection which must not be overlooked. In one and the same class in a school, there may be students whose vernaculars are different, and in such cases it will be difficult to adopt any one of those vernaculars as the medium of instruction. But cases of that kind will not be common, and even where they exist, the great majority of students in the class will be found to have one common vernacular which is the prevailing vernacular of the place, and which may be adopted as the medium of instruction.

The second objection, namely, that the adoption of the vernacular as the medium of instruction in the Secondary stage will retard the progress of higher Education, is I venture to think, more a needless than a real alarm. If English continues to be studied, as it ought be, as a second language, while the other subjects are taught in the vernacular, the comparative ease with which those subjects will be learnt will enable the student to have more spare time and energy than he now has, and he will be able to devote all that to the learning of English better. And the apprehended disadvantage of students having to learn the technical terms of certain subjects in two languages,. namely, first in his vernacular, and then later in English, is so small that it will be more than amply compensated by the advantage of being able to learn those subjects better and more easily in his vernacular. So that the advantages of adopting the vernacular as the medium of instruction will in every way outweigh all possible disadvantages, and there is no real danger of the progress of higher Education being retarded in any manner. On the other hand, the expansion of the vernacular basis of Education will indirectly help the spread of Education in the country.

I would therefore earnestly press the suggestion made above, that the vernacular of the student should as a rule be adopted as the medium of instruction throughout the Secondary stage.

V. Methods of Imparting Education.

The question, what is the true method of imparting Education, has given rise to much difference of opinion, which is the result of differences in views as to the true aim of Education and the true nature of the being to be educated.

If the object of Education be merely to store the learner's mind with knowledge, the method of imparting Education will be for the teacher to go on simply communicating knowledge to the learner who will remain a passive recipient of that knowledge except when answering questions set to see whether the knowledge has been received and retained. But if the object be not merely to store the mind with knowledge, but also to train and develop its powers, the method of imparting Education must be different, and must consist in helping the learner not simply in knowing new facts communicated to him, but also in observing new facts for himself, and in finding out for himself their relations to one another.

Again, if we regard every human being of sound mind and sound body as possessed of indefinite capacity for learning everything and for applying every kind of knowledge, our method of Education will be one uniform method for all students.

But if on the other hand, we accept the view that there are radical differences in the mental capacities of different individuals, our methods of imparting Education will be different for different types of students, and before resorting to coercive measures against any student, we shall have to pause and ascertain whether his want of progress in any subject is due to want of will or want of power to learn.

With the progress of time, our views in matters educational, as in other matters, have undergone important change, new educational principles have been deduced from facts furnished by observation and experiment, and if no royal road to learning has yet been discovered, the ordinary road to it has been made more easy by the removal of unnecessary obstructions in it. Great educators like Rousseau, Pestalozzi, Froebel, and Herbart have entered emphathic protests against old methods of coercion in Education, and have recommended methods for making the receiving of instruction a source of pleasure; while Experimental Psychology has been trying to ascertain the limits of mental capacity for work and the cause and cure of fatigue, in order to prevent learners from being unnecessarily harassed. All this is good within proper limits. But things are proceeding so far and so fast in the direction of ease and relaxation, that the time for counterprotest seems to have arrived; and what I shall say here will be in the nature of warning against the danger of inculcating love of ease and relaxation in methods of Education.

Restraint is an evil, not only because it gives pain, but also because it retards instead of accelarating work and progress. We naturally and instinctively like to be free, and to work freely. But if every one tries to do freely whatever he wishes, no one will be free, because every one will be restrained by all others he comes in contact with. Therefore if restraint is an evil, it is a necessary evil, and the only way of avoiding it, is, by substituting internal restraint, that is self-restraint, for restraint from without. He who can restrain himself, never gives any one else any occasion for restraining him; he is really free from restraint by others; and being free he is truly happy. But that happiness, like every other valuable thing, has to be obtained at some cost. Self restraint has to be learnt after long and laborious practice. It should be one of the chief objects of Education to teach self-restraint. And every educational method which impedes, or interferes in any way with, the formation and growth of habits of self-restraint, must be abandoned as antagonistic to the true aim of Education. We naturally love ease and pleasure; but carried to excess, that love interferes with discipline and self-restraint. While allowing some scope for ease and pleasure, the effort of the teacher should be to guard carefully against any excess. Mr. Sandiford in his admirable book on the "Mental and Physical Life of School Children" has well observed (p. 225)—"The followers of Herbart have allowed interest to become synonymous in meaning with ease and pleasure. Hence the failure of interest as a pedagogic doctrine. Always to obey the dictates of the native interests means the arrest of intellectual progress. The teacher should bear in mind the great satisfaction which comes with the completion of a hard task; and that permanent interests are only developed under the stress of voluntary attention. Children therefore should be given hard tasks, but not so hard as to be beyond their powers from the beginning."

Up to a certain age, to favour physical growth, hard intellectual labour should not be imposed on a child. But at the same time it should be borne in mind that a child takes pleasure in learning new things, if they are taught in a cheerful and not a surly mood, and that a child should be gradually accustomed to take to work and labour and to be able to withdraw from play and pleasure.

The Kindergarten method with all respect for Froebel's honoured name, should be resorted to, if at all, with care and reserve, intelligently and not mechanically.

So again, the rule now followed in some schools, not to teach any subject continuously for more than forty-five minutes, and to allow an interval of five minutes between subject and subject, in order to prevent fatigue, seems to be of questionable wisdom. Boys should not be made to work when they distinctly feel fatigued, for work will not make good progress then. That is no doubt a wise rule in the interests of work; but it is not an equally wise rule in the interests of the workers under training, who are not only to be taught to work, but are also to be taught to work under stress and strain. You may treat them tenderly at school, but the world outside will not treat them so. And if you want to train them for the rough world, you must inure them early to toil and fatigue.

Moreover, rules like the one just mentioned, which are deduced from a few experiments tried upon a few groups of boys, are not likely to be so precise that we should follow them without testing them by observation in particular cases, and even when their operation is attended with inconvenience. Now I do not think that observation has confirmed the view that Bengali boys feel fatigued after an hour with a lesson in language teaching, and I do think it very inconvenient in the Secondary stage, to lay down a hard and fast rule limiting a lesson in language teaching to one hour or less, with a class of thirty boys, so that no boy can have more than two minutes time devoted to him. If each boy is made to read out and explain one or two sentences with the help of the teacher, while other boys go on listening, and this sort of work goes on for a couple of hours, each boy will have some attention paid to him individually, while there will be sufficient variety in the work for each to prevent fatigue.

An important question connected with the method of imparting instruction is, whether students should be taught with or without the assistance of text-books. Opinion is divided upon this question, and the more favoured view seems to be to dispense with text-books as far as possible, because, it is said, we have to teach subjects and not text-books. The reason is good, but the conclusion drawn from it is not correct. True it is that we have to teach subjects and not text-books, but how is a subject to be taught without text-books? If you dispense with text-books, the teacher must prepare notes of lessons for his guidance, and the students must copy out those notes (for they cannot be expected to carry them all in memory) for revision of the lessons at home. And so the teacher's notes, or rather the imperfect copies made by the students of the teacher's notes, will take the place of text-books. It is better far to adopt suitable text-books as guide for the teacher in teaching and for the student in learning a subject.

The objection to text-books is most strenuously urged in regard to the teaching of English. It is said that if text-books are prescribed, students commit to memory the prescribed text-books and the keys to them, without learning English. But if good text-books are prescribed, even committing them to memory will not be altogether unprofitable, as it will enable the student to learn peculiarities of construction and idiom which constitute the chief difficulties in the way of learning English. Keys of course should be carefully discarded, and the student should be made to find out for himself with the aid of a dictionary the meanings of words, and with occasional help from the teacher to make out the meaning of a lesson, and also to notice every peculiarity of construction and idiom that it presents. The careful reading of a small quantity of matter will enable the student to learn more English than the perfunctory reading of a much larger quantity.

Another important point connected with method is, that students should be made to find out and work out things for themselves, instead of the teacher at school or a private tutor at home finding out and working out every thing for them. Suggestive hints and occasional guidance are helpful, but too much assistance is embarrassing and enervating. But if students are to do their own work, it is necessary that the work set for them to do should be moderate in quantity and easy in quality. If you set them lessons too long or too hard, they will not be able to prepare them without the help of private tutors or keys. Every one sees that, and yet in most schools long lessons are invariably set. Perfunctorily going over a large quantity of matter is taken for progress, and the result is that very little is really learnt, and a very bad habit is contracted by students of doing things in a slipshod way, which is injurious to further progress. Unless this pernicious practice of setting long lessons is discontinued, and the use of those mischievous keys which profess to do everything for the learner is discarded, no educational reform will be of any use.

I shall conclude this topic with a few remarks on what is called the Direct Method of teaching a foreign language. It consists in making the student associate in his mind words and sentences of the language he is learning, directly with the things and thoughts they signify, instead of connecting them indirectly with those things and thoughts by translating them into their corresponding words and sentences in his own vernacular. The learning of a language is no doubt more thorough, the more this direct connection of its words and sentences with the things and thoughts they signify is established in the learner's mind. But the real difficulty lies in securing the establishment of this direct connection in all cases. Take the case of a Bengali boy learning English. He begins at an age at which he has already acquired a stock of Bengali words and sentences sufficient for his ordinary purposes, so that when the corresponding English words and sentences are presented to him simultaneously with representations of the things and thoughts they signify (which, by the way, is not always possible), the Bengali equivalents of the English words and sentences will make their appearance in consciousness and will share the attention with those representations, and thus disturb and weaken the direct connection sought to be created. Then again, the connection of the things and thoughts with their English verbal equivalents will be limited to the school hours, and when the boy goes home, the same things and thoughts will be associated with their Bengali verbal equivalents. Thus the force and the frequency of association of the linguistic signs with the things and thoughts they signify, will be insufficient to make the direct method as efficacious as its advocates suppose it to be. It cannot be resorted to as the sole method, but it is undoubtedly a useful supplement to the indirect method of teaching language by translation.

The direct method is not a new thing as its advocates think; it is only the endeavour to make it the exclusive method that is new. Teachers had been using the direct method all along wherever practicable, without giving it the prominence that is now claimed for it, as a famous character once said he had been talking prose all his life without knowing it.

CHAPTER VI.

TESTING OF EDUCATION—EXAMINATIONS.

I come now to the sixth and last head of my discourse, namely, Testing of Education and Examinations.

Education has to be tested, not only for the satisfaction of its recipient and his friends, but also for the benefit of the public at whose expense it is sometimes imparted, and who as the employers of educated and skilled labour may desire to know whether those receiving Education have really acquired the knowledge and skill intended to be imparted.

For small communities of students, teachers themselves may test Education and pronounce judgment on the merits of their pupils without any formal Examination. For large communities of students, that is not possible, for want of sufficient personal knowledge of the teacher regarding the merits of the pupils, and formal Examination becomes necessary. The teacher's pronouncement has this advantage over the ordinary Examination test, that it is based upon a comprehensive view of the student's work during the whole or a large part of his period of studentship, while an Examination is a test of his work for a few hours which is taken as a sample of his whole work. But the teacher's judgment is liable to be taken exception to on the ground of its being biased in favour of his pupils.

All things considered, Examination with all its defects remains the only available test of Education imparted on a large scale. And the practical question is, How to make Examination a proper test of Education? that is, How to fix proper standards for Pass and for Honours? How to frame proper Question Papers? and How properly to examine Answer Papers?

In dealing with these questions, the following remarks of Mr. Latham in the Preface to his elaborate work "On the Action of Examinations" may be usefully borne in mind. "When too much value" says he, "is attached to a place in an Examination test, candidates are rendered morbidly anxious by their fear of disappointing their friends, and teachers are forced for their credit to convey something that can be displayed in an Examination, even though, as is especially the case with young boys, the proper course of teaching must be interfered with to effect this object. On the other hand, when the verdict of Examinations is slighted, as has happened sometimes since the reaction against them began, young people harden themselves against the rightful punishment of their inattention by disparaging the instrument which reveals their deficiencies." I may add that this latter evil is likely to be increased when the disparagement of Examinations proceeds not from disappointed students only but from dissatisfied teachers and professors as well. It is very unfortunate that teachers and professors are dissatisfied with the action of of our University and its Examinations, notwithstanding their having a statutory majority on the Syndicate, and notwithstanding that they have or can, if they wish, always have, the chief hand in the conduct of those Examinations. It is however gratifying and hopeful to find that there are eminent professors and educationists of long and varied Indian experience who take a different attitude.

To the question, How to fix proper standards for Pass and Honours in our Examinations, one uniform answer can hardly be expected. Learned professors whose educational ideals are naturally high, and who are interested in seeing that well qualified students come to them, would fix high standards generally, and especially for the Matriculation Examination. On the other hand, that section of the public who have faith more in the Education which the world gives than in what is received in School or College, will have the standards made low and Examinations made easy. While the majority of the public who, though wishing for the success of our students, are at the same time anxious to maintain the reputation of our Examinations and of our students, would have the standards fixed high enough to prevent their suffering by comparison with those of other Universities, but not too high to make our Examinations unnecessarily stiff. It is this intermediate view that may be adopted as sound, and accepting that view, it cannot be said that our standards are low.

Roughly speaking, the Calcutta University has fixed 36 per cent of the full marks in English, and 30 per cent in other subjects, as the minimum pass marks for its Examinations. This is not a low standard (I speak subject to correction) compared with those of English Universities as far as I have been able to ascertain. Nor are our question papers comparatively easy.

In one respect the Calcutta University is more exacting in its Examinations than many other Universities, and its Examinations should therefore be regarded as comparatively more stiff. It prescribes six subjects for the Matriculation Examination, five for the Intermediate Examinations in Arts and Science, and four for the B. A. Examination, and it insists upon candidates passing in all the subjects at the same time instead of allowing them to take the subjects successively, and pass by compartments as it is called. And passing in all the prescribed subjects simultaneously at one Examination is more difficult, and is proof of the possession of greater mental capacity, than passing in them successively in different Examinations.

The only alteration that I would suggest in our Regulations relating to the standards for Pass and Honours would be, to fix 30 per cent as the minimum pass marks in all the subjects except English, as a broad general rule, and to dispense with the niceties about varying minimum marks in individual subjects and a minimum aggregate for a Pass.

The question,—How to frame proper Question Papers?—is one of considerable difficulty, and involves many very important points for consideration.

A few papers (about a dozen) of which each is to be answered in a few hours (about three) are to test knowledge which has been acquired in two years, and to test capacity which is to last a whole life.

Then they have to distinguish the good from the bad, and the best among the good from the remainder of that group, out of large numbers of students of all possible varieties of mental structure.

They will also indirectly guide teachers in teaching and students in learning their subjects of study in future years.

When questions have to serve so many and such varied purposes, one can never be too careful in framing them, and paper-setters should fully realize the importance of the work entrusted to them. The rules laid down by our University for the guidance of paper-setters and examiners are good so far as they go, but they do not go far enough, and I shall presently suggest one or more additions to them. Rules however can only serve as general guides, and too many minute rules hamper instead of helping work, the success of which must ultimately depend upon the good sense and discrimination of those who have to apply the rules in practice.

The rule requiring the fair distribution of the questions set in any subject over the whole course in that subject and the allowance of some choice of questions to examinees, is intended to give equal advantage to all diligent students, and to prevent any one from gaining or losing by reason of accidentally giving or omitting to give full attention to any particular portion of a subject.

I would suggest that the rule requiring fair distribution of questions over the whole course in a subject should be supplemented by a direction to avoid generally questions that are too minute or too difficult. Such a direction is perhaps implied by the word "fairly" and also by the rule requiring that the qnestions should be so framed as to encourage good methods of work and teaching; but it will be well to have an explicit direction such as I have suggested. I emphasize this point on account of its bearing on an important question relating to methods of study and teaching.

We study a subject partly for the value of the knowledge of the truths it teaches, and partly for the value of the discipline it gives, that is the value of the habits and powers which the study of the subject develops in us. This latter value, in the opinion of many educational experts, has been very much exaggerated, and one of them (Mr. Thorndike) in his work on Teaching calls the common view on the subject. "The superstition of General Training"; but he gives the superstition credit for embodying some truth, for, says he speaking of the teacher, "he may fairly expect improvement but less in amount in abilities closely like that trained," and in another place he adds (p. 245) :—

"Difficulties in studies may prepare students for the difficulties of the world as a whole by cultivating the attitudes of neglect or discomfort, ideals of accomplishing what one sets out to do, and the feeling of dissatisfaction with failure."

We may take it then that we study a subject partly for the value of the knowledge and partly for the value of the discipline which the study gives, and, I may add, more for the latter. For take an instance. Of the many thousand students who have read Trigonometry and Sanskrit, how many are there who profit by, or remember, the formula for the general value of an angle having a given sine, or the aphorisms giving the different uses of the common word, *Atha*. They are however, or can be made, useful in teaching valuable lifelong lessons—the former, the lesson that things very different from one another may be brought under one form of expression, and the latter, that a thing apparently one in form may serve many different purposes. But such useful lessons are always buried beneath heaps of useless explanations and copious examples with which the attention of the learner is wholly occupied. It cannot be right, in any general Examination, to set a question paper on any subject, containing minute questions the answers to which none but an expert in the subject would care to remember in after life. The only ground upon which the setting of minute questions may be sought to be justified is, that as our memory of things gradually fades away with time, unless minute details are remembered at the time of Examination which is shortly after they are learnt, even broad principles will be forgotten in after life. But the soundness of this argument is more apparent than real.

The truth is that the retention of a thing in memory varies as the intensity of our attention to it, and the frequency of its repetition ; so that if the broad principles of a subject are made to occupy the whole of our attention without a good part of it being shared, as is often the case, by minute details, and if the broad principles alone are placed before us oftener than they can be when part of our time is occupied with presentation of minute details, both intensity of attention and frequency of repetition will help the retention of broad principles in memory. Minute questions should therefore be discarded except where they bear closely upon broad principles. Questions that are too difficult should also, as a rule, be discarded, but every paper should contain one or two such questions to enable the best students to show their exceptional merit, and to make the Examination a test for discriminating the best from the average.

The reason given in favour of setting long papers is, that as Examination is a test not only of knowledge but also of capacity, it is only a long paper that can test a student's capacity, that is, readiness and resourcefulness, whereas with a short paper, even the less capable may slowly and laboriously work out a great deal. That is true, but it is true only within certain limits, and if those limits are exceeded, a different result might follow, just as a function may go on increasing with the variable up to a certain limit, after which it may begin to decrease though the variable may go on increasing. A singular illustration of this is furnished by the fact that Kelvin was not the Senior Wrangler of his year. Speaking of Cambridge, his biographer Sir W. Ramsay says, "Where the examination system was in full swing, and to the disgrace of the examiners, Thomson was not the Senior Wrangler; he was not regarded as the best Mathematician of his year; and this inspite of the remark made by one of his examiners that 'the Senior Wrangler was not fit to cut pencils for Thomson.' It is known that success in this examination depends largely on rapidity in writing, and on accuracy of memory, rather than on originality; and the tale is told that on Thomson's coach or tutor asking him why he had spent so much time in answering a particular question, he replied that he had to think it all out from first principles. But it is a problem of your own discovery, said the coach. Thomson had to confess that he had quite forgotten his own handwork, and that while his competitor had learnt the answer by heart, Thomson had to rediscover the solution."

While therefore a question paper should not be too short, it must not be too long either.

There are two or three common faults which question papers are liable to fall into, and which call for a passing notice.

One of these is the fault of being unusual and unexpected. It arises from an apprehension on the part of the paper setter lest his paper be considered easy by reason of the questions being, not easy but ordinary and such as would be expected, so that most of the examinees would be prepared to answer them. This is a mistaken and mischievous view.

If students by unfair means ascertain the particular questions set, and come prepared to answer them without preparing their subjects generally, that is certainly wrong. But if students by diligent and thoughtful study come prepared to answer all ordinary questions that they expected, there is nothing wrong in that. On the contrary, if after proper study they find that the papers set are unusual, and contain questions which could not have been expected, that would be clearly wrong. The object of an Examination is to test the merits of the examinees, not to take them by surprise. The ground on which unusual and unexpected questions are sought to be justified is this, that if questions that are usual and expected are set, students will come prepared with their answers got by heart, and so the Examination will be a test of memory only, and not of intelligence.

But if students are prepared to answer all the usual, that is, important, questions in their subjects, that is as good as their knowing the subjects. Unintelligent memorizing is bad, but the memorizing of a whole course in a subject without understanding it, is not a likely thing. And if all the important parts of a subject are understood and remembered, that ought to be considered enough. "It is" as a distinguished educationist (Mr. Thorndike) remarks "fashionable now a days to decry memory as a sort of cheap slavey of the intellect, a 'skeleton in the closet' of teaching, not fit to be mentioned in the polite society of apperception, interest, reasoning and the rest. In the laudable effort to cure school work of the error of trusting every thing to verbal memory, writers on teaching have made the mistake of the surgeon who cured a sprained ankle by cutting off the leg. Indeed the trouble was not with memory, but with what was remembered—words only. We surely must not cut a man's leg off because he walks into danger on them. If a fact is understood, the better it is remembered, the better off we are." (Principles of Teaching, p. 124).

I think there ought to be a rule against the setting of unusual questions. It need not be embodied in the Regulations, as that will give the rule undue rigidity, but it should be in the nature of a direction by the Syndicate for the guidance of paper setters.

Another fault in question papers which should be guarded against is mannerism. This was singularly noticeable in the papers set by an eminent antiquarian and Sanskrit scholar. In a paper on Bengali Poetry (Krittibas's Ramayana being the text-book), examinees were asked to trace the route of Rama from Ayodhya to Dandaka, and in a paper on Bengali Prose (a Bengali translation of Rollin's Ancient History being the text-book) one of the questions was—"Who removed the obelisks of Sesostris from Heptonomis?"

Scholars of striking individuality will always have their mannerism, but papers set at general Examinations should be as free from such peculiarities as possible.

The last fault that should be noticed is pedantry, the outcome of a desire to give an appearance of artistic excellence to the paper. A good question paper is no doubt a work of art, and gives ample scope for exercise of the useful art of making it fulfil all its manifold requirements, which is enough to engross the entire attention of the paper setter.

It remains now to consider the question—How properly to examine answer papers?

One simple answer to the question would be, that in order to have answer papers properly examined, we should appoint good examiners and leave them free to exercise their judgment without being fettered by any rules. But such a course will not be practicable even if it was quite safe, because the number of answer papers corresponding to each question paper at some of the Examinations comes up to several thousands, so that to bring out the results within a reasonable time, we have to appoint more examiners than one to examine the answers to each question paper, and if each examiner is left free to exercise his judgment without being guided by any rule, examinees whose papers are looked over by a lenient examiner will have an advantage over those whose papers fall in the hands of a more strict examiner.

That would hardly be just, especially for Examinations at which successful candidates are placed in different grades according to the marks obtained by them, and scholarships are awarded also according to those marks.

Something must be done to secure uniformity of marking. And what the Calcutta University does, is, to appoint in each subject, a head examiner who fixes a method of awarding marks in consultation with the examiners under him, and supervises their work to see that that method is exactly followed.

At first sight this would appear sufficient to secure uniformity in the method of marking and to do full justice to all examinees. But in reality it has been found that that is not so. Our system may have secured uniformity of marking, but it is more than doubtful whether it has ensured justice for examinees. A remarkable instance came to notice in the course of an inquiry into the causes of a very high percentage of failures at the Entrance Examination some years ago. One of the questions in History required examinees to give a short account of the life of Buddha. The head examiner settled that a full answer to the question should refer to certain points, five or six in number, and the marks assigned to the question were allotted to those five or six points in a certain way, and there was a direction to the examiners that certain grammatical mistakes in the answers should entail certain deductions in the marks. Now one of the candidates had omitted to notice some of those points, and had committed some grammatical mistakes, and for those errors of omission and commission, he lost so many marks that he got either no marks or very insignificant marks for his answer, which though faulty in its parts, was yet when taken as a whole entitled to fair marks. But the method of marking adopted in that case made the importance of the parts superior to that of the whole, furnishing an illustration of Cantor's famous paradox that the whole is sometimes less than its parts.

Some educationists are of opinion that the above mentioned method, which may be called the analytical method or method of marking by dividing an answer into its component parts, should be replaced by the synthetic method or method of marking by taking an answer as a whole and awarding marks to it according to the impression it leaves on the examiner's mind. But such an impression would be different on different minds, and personal equation will be a dominant factor. It is true that in the analytical method too, personal equation will come into play in the awarding of marks for each component element; but the component elements will have been expressly settled before-hand and will be the same for all the examiners concerned, whereas in the synthetic method they are not so settled, but are only vaguely present in their minds, and may not be the same for all. So that the personal element, though present in both, is a much less potent factor in the analytic than in the synthetic method.

I do not think it would be quite safe to adopt what I have called the synthetic method in lieu of the analytic in large Examinations. I would suggest a combination of the two methods as the only way of minimizing the errors of both. And the combined method may be worked out thus :

Determine first the marks to be assigned to an answer by the analytic method, determine next what marks it should get in the synthetic method ; and take the mean of the two as the final award. Very often the two methods will lead to the same result ; it will be only occasionally that they will differ ; and the mean will not always be to the advantage of the examinee. For it is just as possible that the answer taken as a whole may impress the examiner less favourably than the parts when taken separately, as the reverse.

The application of the combined method may be indicated on the answer paper by adding to the marks assigned to an answer in the analytic method such positive or negative marks (if any) as will make the result equal to the mean marks mentioned above. This may slightly increase the quantity of the work of examiners, but it will greatly improve the quality of the work.